MACBETH DID IT

A COMEDY IN THREE ACTS
BY JOHN PATRICK

DRAMATISTS
PLAY SERVICE
INC.

MACBETH DID IT
Copyright © Renewed 2000, Bradley Wayne Strauman, Steven Rehl,
co-executors of John Patrick's estate
Copyright © 1972, John Patrick
Copyright © 1971, John Patrick
as an unpublished dramatic composition

All Rights Reserved

CAUTION: Professionals and amateurs are hereby warned that performance of MACBETH DID IT is subject to payment of a royalty. It is fully protected under the copyright laws of the United States of America, and of all countries covered by the International Copyright Union (including the Dominion of Canada and the rest of the British Commonwealth), and of all countries covered by the Pan-American Copyright Convention, the Universal Copyright Convention, the Berne Convention, and of all countries with which the United States has reciprocal copyright relations. All rights, including professional/amateur stage rights, motion picture, recitation, lecturing, public reading, radio broadcasting, television, video or sound recording, all other forms of mechanical or electronic reproduction, such as CD-ROM, CD-I, DVD, information storage and retrieval systems and photocopying, and the rights of translation into foreign languages, are strictly reserved. Particular emphasis is placed upon the matter of readings, permission for which must be secured from the Author's agent in writing.

The nonprofessional stage performance rights in MACBETH DID IT are controlled exclusively by DRAMATISTS PLAY SERVICE, INC., 440 Park Avenue South, New York, NY 10016. No nonprofessional performance of the Play may be given without obtaining in advance the written permission of DRAMATISTS PLAY SERVICE, INC., and paying the requisite fee.

Inquiries concerning all other rights should be addressed to Dramatists Play Service, Inc., 440 Park Avenue South, New York, NY 10016.

SPECIAL NOTE
Anyone receiving permission to produce MACBETH DID IT is required to give credit to the Author as sole and exclusive Author of the Play on the title page of all programs distributed in connection with performances of the Play and in all instances in which the title of the Play appears for purposes of advertising, publicizing or otherwise exploiting the Play and/or a production thereof. The name of the Author must appear on a separate line, in which no other name appears, immediately beneath the title and in size of type equal to 50% of the size of the largest, most prominent letter used for the title of the Play. No person, firm or entity may receive credit larger or more prominent than that accorded the Author.

YE CAST

JUANITO	Theater janitor
LARRY RENCHER	Director
JILL SEARS	His assistant
EFFIE	First Witch
CLARA	Second Witch
MARY LOU STEINER	Third Witch
BIFF	First Murderer and Soldier
CURTIS HOGY	Stage hand
DUKE MARLBORO	Stage hand
LOUISE	Witches' understudy
ANGIE	Witches' understudy
RALPH	The Porter
DOLLY DIBBLE	Lady Macbeth
EMERSON DIBBLE	Her husband
RODRIQUES	Juanito's uncle
ROSITA	His girl friend
DIXIE DELANEY	Lady-in-waiting
DOCTOR GOLDMAN	The Doctor
HORACE MULLIGAN	McDuff
THORTON	Stage hand
ERIC	Photographer

NOBLEMEN, SOLDIERS, MESSENGERS, and OTHER APPARITIONS

ACT I
"Casting"
SCENE: Community Theatre Stage

ACT II
"Rehearsal"
SCENE 1: The same. A week later
"Coffee Break"
SCENE 2: The same. Ten minutes later

ACT III
"Picture Call"
SCENE 1: The same. Weeks later
"Opening Night"
SCENE 2: The same. Ten minutes before curtain

MACBETH DID IT was first presented by The Vagabond Players (The State Theatre of North Carolina, Robroy Farquhar, Managing Director) at the Flat Rock Playhouse, Flat Rock, North Carolina, in July, 1972. It was directed by the author, the designer was Walter O'Rourke, and the costumes were by Walter Williamson. The assistant to the director was Neal Poole. The cast, in order of appearance, was as follows:

JUANITO	John Batson
LARRY RENCHER	Ralph Redpath
JILL SEARS	Sally Nall
EFFIE	Helen Bragdon
CLARA	Donna Drake
MARY LOU STEINER	Johanna Erlenbach
BIFF	Robin Farquhar
CURTIS HOGG	David Novak
DUKE MARLBORO	Stephen Camp
LOUISE	Susan Shashy
ANGIE	Cathy Friedman
RALPH	Ken Bauer
DOLLY DIBBLE	Kate Bertram
EMERSON DIBBLE	Walter Williamson
RODRIQUES (Juanito's uncle)	Donald Ezell
ROSITA	Ellen Kelly
DIXIE DELANEY	Dyann Beaty
DR. GOLDMAN	Ed Oster
HORACE MULLIGAN (McDuff)	Tom Campbell

MACBETH DID IT

ACT I

PLACE: *The bare stage of any local community theatre.*
TIME: *The present.*

AT RISE: *The curtain is already up as the audience comes in. The bare stage is seen with flats and heating pipes and chairs in the background. There is a door Upstage that leads to the green room or the dressing rooms. There is also a stage door opening onto the street.*

While the audience is being seated, Juanito Hernandez, the theatre janitor, carpenter, and general handyman is seen sweeping up the stage. He is Puerto Rican or Mexican of indeterminate age and education. He pushes a flat floor broom lethargically and sweeps bits of crumpled paper into a dust pan. He turns and crosses again, the papers falling unnoticed from the dust pan held behind him.

At the customary curtain time, the house lights dim and Larry Rencher, the Little Theatre director, comes in from the backstage door. He carries scripts and a clip-board.

LARRY. Como esta, Juanito?

JUANITO. Bien, amigo.

LARRY. Is this as many chairs as we've got? (*Crosses R. to chair and puts scripts down.*)

JUANITO. Rest broke hop. No good for sit.

LARRY. (*Starts collecting stacked chairs.*) I'll need a table. Will you set a table and chair here for me, please? (*Points.*)

JUANITO. (*Stands.*) No got.

LARRY. We've got a card table somewhere. We used it in "Arsenic and Old Lace." Look in props.

JUANITO. You know ole fat lady Meezus Meeler? She already taken him to her house. Is no more here.

LARRY. Well, it belonged to her. (*Looks around.*) See if you can get me a box or something. (*Collects chairs from both wings and*

sets them up on each side of stage with a single row U. C. in preparation for the auditions. He also gets a couple of chairs pre-set down the stage steps at front of audience.)
JUANITO. (*Gets orange crate L. for the script table.*) We do fonny play again?
LARRY. Well, I wouldn't exactly call it funny. We're going to do "Macbeth" next. (*Adds.*) By Shakespeare.
JUANITO. Heez fonny? (*Follows Larry as he sets chairs.*)
LARRY. Let's hope not.
JUANITO. Nobody no come if no for make laughing, I theenk maybe.
LARRY. You'll like this play. It's got witches and a ghost and several murders.
JUANITO. My keeds—they crazy for weetches.
LARRY. You can bring them to dress rehearsal. How many kids you got now?
JUANITO. Eseex (*Six. Note: Most Spanish-speaking people put an "es" in front of an "S."*) Too many I think.
LARRY. How's the rest of your family?
JUANITO. You know my honcle?
LARRY. Rodriques?
JUANITO. (*Nods.*) Weeth the one eye. Ju know de reever? Ju know heez belly-button? He fell in it up to it.
LARRY. What was he doing at the river?
JUANITO. Heez got heemself a gurl, ju know. They goin' to de reever to looking for estrawberry. I theenk maybe they looking for trouble.
LARRY. Who's the girl?
JUANITO. Ju know Rosita Montenegro? Ju know her teets? Like theez. (*Makes a gesture as if holding a watermelon.*) Sum keed!
LARRY. Each to his own. (*Starts distributing coffee cans around chairs to use as ash trays.*)
JUANITO. Heez crazy for her. Espending all heez money.
LARRY. Why doesn't he marry her?
JUANITO. Heez afraid of her hoosbon. (*Follows without offering to help.*)
LARRY. Oh—she married?
JUANITO. You know what theez crazy Rosita esay to my honcle? She es-say—Why we doan keel my hoosbon?
LARRY. Kill him! What does your uncle say?

JUANITO. He esay—I no like for keel nobody.
LARRY. He's right.
JUANITO. All de time she doan leave heem alone. She esay—you doan like me for make marriage. You only like me for you-know-why-we-go-to-de-reever.
LARRY. You tell your uncle to get rid of that girl.
JUANITO. Push her head under de reever?
LARRY. No—no. Just drop her.
JUANITO. On de head?
LARRY. Give her up. She's no good for him.
JUANITO. She doan lat heem. She esay, why you doan keel my hoosbon? She esay—in heez mattress is hiding feefty dollar. She esay, eez easy—we keel heem—we take heez money and we ronning away. Sheez crazy.
LARRY. You tell him fifty dollars isn't worth committing murder for. He doesn't need a woman that bad.
JUANITO. But he needs de *money*.
LARRY. Juanito—that's exactly what Macbeth is all about. Greed and murder. You bring him to see a rehearsal.
JUANITO. Theez Macbeth—sheez about Espan-ish peoples?
LARRY. In spirit. It's about what happens when intelligent people let their emotions run away with them.
JUANITO. I bring heem. Eez ho-K if heez bringing Rosita?
LARRY. Why not? I'd like to see her.
JUANITO. Som keed.
LARRY. So was Lady Macbeth. (*The stage door in the background, that leads off into the street, opens and Jill Sears, an attractive, vital and straight forward girl in her early twenties, comes in with a paper bag in one hand and a stack of books under her arm. She comes down to Larry,* R.)
JILL. Hi, slugger. Sorry I'm late. Hi, Juanito.
LARRY. It's all right. No one's here yet. (*Juanito exits.*)
JILL. (*Gives him a furtive kiss and starts arranging books on makeshift table at first chair in row,* R.) Some last minute dictation. If I didn't need that job to pay for my car, I'd tell Mr. Emerson Dibble to take his Dibble and Company and— (*Changes her mind.*) Never mind. I know you hate vulgarity.
LARRY. Only in public.
JILL. Then I had to drop mother off at her weekly seance. I don't know why she thinks father is going to speak to her from beyond

the grave. He never spoke to her when he was alive. (*Takes a hamburger out of the sack.*) I didn't even have time for dinner. (*Turns to him.*) Want a bite?
LARRY. No thanks. I've eaten. (*Crosses* U. *to leave coat on chair.*)
JILL. I didn't mean the hamburger. I meant me.
LARRY. Not with onions.
JILL. I know *your* tastes. Raw.
LARRY. Not in the theater.
JILL. Larry, can I ask you something? (*Puts her arm around his neck.*)
LARRY. Yes. I love you.
JILL. I know that. What I want to know is—*why* are you doing "Macbeth"!
LARRY. (*Breaks away, annoyed.*) I've told you! We have a cultural obligation to the community in which we live.
JILL. Nuts. Last time we fulfilled that obligation, we emptied the theater.
LARRY. Camille was a critical success! (*Crosses to put script on chair,* L.)
JILL. Half the audience didn't even wait for her to die.
LARRY. Jill—if you don't want to work on this production—skip it. I'll find somebody else. (*Crosses back to her,* C.)
JILL. No. I love helping out here. I just think you're making a mistake. Who can you get to play Lady Macbeth?
LARRY. I've already got someone.
JILL. Who?
LARRY. Well, you don't like her. That's why I think maybe you ought to duck this one.
JILL. Look—I get along with my mother, I can get along with anybody. Who?
LARRY. Mrs. Emerson Dibble. (*Crosses in front of her toward his clip-board,* R.)
JILL. (*Turns.*) Dolly? That pot of poisoned honey?
LARRY. (*Turns back to her.*) Look—she may not be physically right but she's a capable actress.
JILL. Well, heaven knows she's capable of murder. You must be out of your cotton-picking mind.
LARRY. Just because you don't like working for Emerson is no reason to project your hostility on Dolly. (*Crosses to his chair,* R.)

JILL. Oh yes, it is. If she paid more attention to him, he'd pay less attention to me.
LARRY. Well, she's going to play Lady Macbeth. (*Sits and refers to notes.*)
JILL. She'll stink. The "Mobile Menace."
LARRY. Look—you saw her play the Jewish mother in "Majority of One." She was very believable.
JILL. Believable! Her attempts at a Jewish accent put the Jews back fifty years. And, of course, I mean light years.
LARRY. She broke attendance records.
JILL. Sure. If you count the tickets she gave away.
LARRY. (*Rises and crosses to Jill, takes her hands.*) Jill—Emerson Dibble has just bought this whole block, including this theater. There's talk of tearing the building down. As long as Dolly can act here, the building will remain standing.
JILL. No, it won't. The audience will tear it down.
LARRY. And in addition and furthermore—as the politicians say—I need my job here for just one more year.
JILL. Why didn't you say you were playing politics? I'm not above fraud and collusion. "Macbeth" is a beautiful play and Dolly's ideal. (*Kisses him.*)
LARRY. *She* wants to play it. *I* want another year's experience here as resident director before I tackle New York.
JILL. Are you going to take me with you?
LARRY. Is this blackmail?
JILL. Would you prefer murder?
LARRY. I'd prefer to have you help me. It's going to be tough enough getting this classic on its feet. (*Crosses to his chair, R. and sits.*)
JILL. Let's get in my car after auditions and go out and get crocked.
LARRY. I'll be ready. God, how I hate auditions! Do you want to know who else I've cast?
JILL. (*Gets her clip-board.*) I know where you've cast me.
LARRY. (*Reads list.*) Well, after Dolly, I have Horace Mulligan as Macbeth, Thane of Glamis.
JILL. You're kidding.
LARRY. (*Explodes.*) Are you going to help me or not!
JILL. (*Standing at C.*) But he's a butcher. Mulligan's Meats. You

can't cast Macbeth the butcher with Mulligan the butcher. You're dead.

LARRY. He takes out a lot of advertising in our program. And he's a pretty good actor.

JILL. He's a lousy butcher. Alright. I swallow his veal, I can swallow this. (*Writes it on her clip board.*)

LARRY. Lady McDuff—Flora Shannon.

JILL. That's not bad. When did she get out of the hospital?

LARRY. (*Vaguely.*) Oh, last month. It was twins again. Anyhow, she's on her feet and she's reliable.

JILL. On her feet—yes.

LARRY. Then I thought it would be interesting to have Dr. Goldman play the doctor in the sleep walking scene.

JILL. (*Crosses to face him.*) But he's a dentist. Lady Macbeth is having trouble with her conscience—not her teeth.

LARRY. I know, but he's Dolly Dibble's dentist and she asked me.

JILL. O.K. Who else has their hooks in you?

LARRY. Well, Duncan will be Otis Taylor.

JILL. Oh, Larry, he's so old. He'll die on stage before he gets killed. (*Crosses c., imitating a feeble old man.*)

LARRY. I know but he's sweet and he's always supported the theater. And, poor guy, he has diabetes.

JILL. (*Writes it down.*) O.K. Duncan played by Rip Van Winkle Taylor without sugar.

LARRY. Lincoln Harris will be McDuff.

JILL. (*Looks up.*) Larry dear—McDuff was *not* colored.

LARRY. I know but we've been criticized for not being more integrated.

JILL. O.K. Lincoln Harris as McDuff—first black king of Scotland. (*Writes it down.*)

LARRY. And the rest—witches, Soldiers and messengers—we'll cast tonight. (*Rises and calls out over the audience.*) Juanito! (*To Jill.*) You suppose no one is going to turn out? (*Crosses c. to peer into auditorium.*)

JILL. Seven-thirty auditions always mean eight. People have to eat, you know.

LARRY. Well, somebody should have shown up. Unless there's a boycott of Shakespeare. (*Juanito comes in from the wings with one more chair.*)

JUANITO. I think no more chairs.

LARRY. That's all right. Juanito—hasn't anybody showed up? I set auditions for seven-thirty.
JUANITO. (*Drops chair.*) Son of a gun! I forget. (*Races to the stage steps.*)
LARRY. Where are you going?
JUANITO. I forget to unlock front door. Son of a gun! (*Goes down the steps into aisle and runs toward lobby.*)
LARRY. (*Calls after him.*) Turn the lights on in the lobby before you open the house doors. (*Then adds.*) And tell everybody if they've brought their dogs to please leave them in their cars.
JILL. (*Disgusted.*) "Macbeth"! Where are you going to rent costumes?
LARRY. We're not. We're going to make them ourselves. (*Arranges* u. *chairs.*)
JILL. Here we go—burlap again.
LARRY. Jill, if you're going to be downbeat—let someone else take over. I can't handle you and a bunch of amateurs too.
JILL. Oh, no—I want to stick around and see Dolly Dibble make her entrance opening night, crocked to the gills. (*Sits with her notes,* R.)
LARRY. She's on the wagon. She told me.
JILL. Kidneys, I hope.
LARRY. She's losing weight. Lay off her. After all, she's President of the Board. (*Looks out over audience as people start to file down the aisles and up stage steps right and left.*) Well, looks like a good turn out. (*Calls.*) Right down here, folks. Thank you for coming. Sorry to keep you waiting out there in the rain. Come up on stage, please. Hi, Louise. Be careful of those steps. Last show we did, someone fell in the pit. We still haven't found him. Hi, Mrs. Williams—haven't seen you since "Harvey." Sit down anywhere, please. I'm afraid some of you will have to stand. Hi, Horace— how's the undertaking business?
HORACE. Slow.
LARRY. Well, that's life. Hi, Effie. Haven't seen you since "Curious Savage." There'd be something wrong if you didn't show up.
EFFIE. (*A delightful, elderly woman with warmth and humor.*) Fred says I ought to move my trunk over here.
LARRY. What are you going to read for this time, dear? Lady Macbeth is cast.

EFFIE. Oh, I thought I'd try out for one of the witches. I've got my own broom. (*Laughs raucously.*)
LARRY. You could be a witch and understudy Lady Macbeth.
EFFIE. Always an understudy—never a star.
LARRY. We'll find something for you. Grab a seat and I'll get to you as soon as I can. (*She sits in first chair* D. L. *Larry turns to a group of self-conscious young men as they file up on stage in a group,* L.) Hi, fellows. Will you all just stand over stage right behind the chairs? We're short of seats.
BIFF. (*One of the youths.*) Which is stage right?
LARRY. (*Points.*) Stage right is to the left for actors.
BIFF. That's wild. O.K. to smoke? (*They sit* U. *of Effie.*)
LARRY. Tobacco, yes. (*To the group as they settle themselves into the circle of chairs.*) Everybody—it's all right to smoke but use the coffee cans you'll find next to the chairs. (*Calls to back of house.*) Anybody else, Juanito.?
JUANITO. No bodies more I think no.
LARRY. Good. Leave the doors open. (*Paces* U. *above the group.*) Well, we can get started. Welcome, everyone. First let me say— those of you who are not cast tonight, if you want to be with the show, we can always use you backstage. How many here would be willing to be in props, costumes, lighting or any other jobs on the show? Raise your hands. (*All hands go up.*) Good. That's the community spirit I like to see. As you know, for our third production this season, we're doing "Macbeth." (*Jill groans. Juanito returns to stage and disappears into wings.*) Oh, I think most of you know Jill Sears. She's production assistant. Any problems—see her. Now. Most of the leads have been cast. Tonight we're looking for soldiers, ghosts, murderers and witches. And witches' understudies. Who's here for witches? (*Several hands go up. Crosses* D. C.) Effie—we'll start with you, if you're ready.
EFFIE. (*Rises.*) I'm as ready as I'll ever be. (*Comes* D. C. *and grins.*) I can tap dance if that'll help.
JILL. It would help *me*.
LARRY. (*Hands her a script.*) Take Scene Three. Scene One doesn't give you much of an opportunity.
EFFIE. Wait'll I get my glasses. (*Rummages through her bag.*)
LARRY. You read with her, Jill.
JILL. Which witch?

LARRY. Effie will read first witch. You read the other two. (*Turns to Effie.*) Find them yet?
EFFIE. No. But I found an earring I lost. (*Looks up.*) I've left them home.
LARRY. Here—try mine.
EFFIE. (*Puts on Larry's glasses.*) You read with these! (*She holds the book at arm's length.*)
LARRY. Can you see with them?
EFFIE. (*Book close to nose.*) Yes. But I'm not sure I can breathe.
JILL. Page four. Bottom of the page.
EFFIE. (*Flipping pages.*) I always get so nervous. (*Holds the book so close, her face is obscured. Only her lips are seen.*)
LARRY. Just read. I don't expect a performance. (*Goes down steps inso aisle to listen and watch.*) Go ahead, Jill.
JILL. (*Crosses to read with Effie.*) Thunder. Enter three witches. First witch. "Where has thou been, sister?" Second witch. "Killing swine." Third witch. "Sister, where thou?" (*Looks up and waits.*) That's your cue, Effie.
EFFIE. (*Jumps.*) Oh. Will you give it to me again?
JILL. "Sister, where thou?"
EFFIE. (*Reads laboriously, only her lips showing below the book.*) "A sailor's wife had chestnuts in her lap. And munch'd. And munch'd. And munch'd. Give me—give me—" (*Turns the page.*)
BIFF. (*From sidelines.*) Give me liberty or give me death.
LARRY. (*From aisle.*) Please! Boys. No clowning. This is tragedy.
EFFIE. (*Finds next page.*) I've got it. (*Reads.*) "Give me—" (*Corrects herself.*) "Give me," quoth I: Aroint thee, witch! the rump-fed ronyon—" (*Looks up.*) What's a ronyon?
LARRY. I don't know. Go on.
EFFIE. (*Pulls book up to her face again.*) "—the rump-fed ronyon cries. Her husband's to Aleppo gone, master o' the Tiger: But in a sieve I'll thither sail. And like a rat without a tail, I'll do, I'll do, and I'll do."
LARRY. That's enough, Effie. You'll do.
EFFIE. For what? (*Hands glasses back to him over footlights.*) I was terrible.
LARRY. You were fine. You're a witch. Rehearsals start Thursday. (*Effie returns to her seat.*) Who's next for witches?
JILL. (*Reads from her list.*) Angie Schoemaker and Louise Hock. (*To Larry.*) Why not read them together?

LARRY. (*To the girls sitting* U. C.) Girls, you want to take a crack at this now?
ANGIE. (*Rises and comes center with Louise.*) If you say.
LOUISE. Why not? It's raining out. (*Jill hands them sides.*)
LARRY. (*From audience.*) Take top of page seven. Don't try for performance. I just want to get a sense of projection. Jill will cue you. This is for the second and third witch.
LOUISE. Which am I?
LARRY. Take your choice.
ANGIE. You say.
LARRY. (*Points to Louise.*) Read third witch. O.K. Go ahead. Cue them, Jill.
JILL. (*Reads.*) "Hail, Thane of Glamis!" (*Looks up. There is silence. Angie looks up.*)
ANGIE. Now?
LARRY. That's your cue, dear.
ANGIE. Oh.
JILL. (*Repeats.*) "Hail, Thane of Glamis!"
ANGIE. (*Reads.*) "Hail!"
LOUISE. (*Reads.*) "Hail!"
LARRY. (*Quickly.*) That's fine, girls! Thank you. Don't leave. Who's next?
LOUISE. Could I try it again? I can get more feeling.
LARRY. No need. We can probably use you as understudy witches. O.K., kids?
LOUISE. (*To Angie.*) O.K. with you?
ANGIE. You say.
LOUISE. O.K. (*They go back to sit and watch.*)
LARRY. (*To Jill.*) Who else have you got?
JILL. You want witches or ghosts?
LARRY. Let's get the witches set first. (*To group.*) Any more witches here? (*A couple of hands go up. Larry points to a pretty girl in a blue dress. It is cut as high and as low as the law allows.*) Miss—in the blue dress—will you come center stage, please? (*She walks sexily to* C. *and takes a pose. Everyone watches eagerly. Larry calls over to Jill from the audience.*) What's her name, Jill?
JILL. (*Consults her list.*) I don't know which one she is.
LARRY. (*To girl.*) Will you give her your name, please?
GIRL. I gave it to her once. (*Sweetly to Jill.*) Mary Lou Steiner.
JILL. (*Checking it off.*) Sorry I didn't remember you.

MARY LOU. Girls never do.
LARRY. So—you want to be a witch? (*Comes down to stand at footlights facing Mary Lou.*)
MARY LOU. I am a witch.
LARRY. Have you done anything for us before?
MARY LOU. Not for you personally.
LARRY. You seem too pretty to be a convincing witch.
MARY LOU. Want to be convinced?
LARRY. Would you tell us what experience you've had?
MARY LOU. Here? In front of everyone? (*People laugh, the boys whistle.*)
LARRY. In the theater.
MARY LOU. (*Counts off on her fingers.*) Well—I played Joan in "St. Joan," Suzie in "Suzie Wong," Opal in "Everybody Loves Opal," Mame in "Auntie Mame," Eileen in "My Sister Eileen," Ruth in "Dear Ruth," Mary in "Little Mary Sunshine," and in "Susan and God," I played God. Shall I go on?
JILL. Once you've played God—what's left?
LARRY. Where did you do all those!
MARY LOU. Bennington. I majored in drama. I've just come home.
LARRY. Do you live here?
MARY LOU. (*Importantly.*) My father is Sheriff Steiner.
LARRY. Oh. (*Repeats—a little higher.*) Oh. Well, Miss Steiner, we'll be happy to use you.
MARY LOU. Thank you.
LARRY. But the witch isn't much of a part.
MARY LOU. I'll make something of it.
LARRY. I'm really embarrassed to offer it to you.
MARY LOU. At least it's a foot in the door.
LARRY. We won't ask you to read. Not with your experience.
MARY LOU. Oh, but I want to read.
LARRY. Oh. Of course, Miss Steiner. Jill, let her read.
JILL. (*Crosses to stand at her side.*) Take the second scene in Act Four. The third witch has a long speech at the top of page 56.
MARY LOU. Are you going to cue me, dear?
JILL. Why, did you want to be both witches? (*Hands her book.*) Here.
MARY LOU. (*Waves the book aside.*) Oh, I don't need that. Just start with "double double." (*Crosses D. C.*)
JILL. (*Glares at her but reads cue line.*) "Double, double, toil and

trouble; Fire burn and cauldron bubble." (*Looks up expectantly. Mary Lou proceeds to recite the third witch's speech flawlessly out to the audience.*)
MARY LOU.
>"Scale of dragon, tooth of wolf,
>Witches' mummy, maw and gulf
>Gall of goat, and slips of yew
>Silver'd in the moon's eclipse,
>Nose of Turk and Tartar's lips,
>Finger of birth-strangled babe
>Ditch-deliver'd by a drab,
>Make the gruel thick and slab:
>Double, double, toil and trouble;
>Fire burn and cauldron bubble."

(*Tosses her hair back triumphantly.*) Would you like more of this crud?
LARRY. That's splendid, Miss Steiner. (*Everyone applauds.*)
JILL. The next line reads: "Cool it with a baboon's blood,"
MARY LOU. I know—*dear.*
LARRY. You'll be a valuable addition to our theater here, Miss Steiner. Have you played "Macbeth" before?
MARY LOU. No. I *directed* it.
LARRY. (*Stunned.*) Oh. Oh, well, our rehearsals start Thursday. We rehearse at night. Seven-thirty to ten.
MARY LOU. That's all right. I'm a night person.
LARRY. Thank you. (*Mary Lou walks sexily back to her seat, u. c.*)
JILL. Next witch? (*As Jill looks at her list, the street door backstage opens and Mrs. Emerson Dibble, a rather large, over-dressed woman carrying a small dog, enters. Whether this actress is cast big or small, she is definitely miscast as Lady Macbeth. She calls through the door, sweetly. She has a thick Southern accent.*)
DOLLY. Pick me up on your way back, Emerson. I'll only be a few minutes. (*Turns and sees group, claps her hand over her mouth.*) Oh. I'm sorry. I'm interrupting. (*Gasps in mock remorse.*)
LARRY. (*Jumps up on stage to greet his star.*) It's all right. Come in, Dolly. We're just getting started with readings. (*Goes to her and kisses her on the cheek.*)
DOLLY. I thought I'd drop by and listen in if I'm not in the way. Emerson has to take some drunk Elks home. Will I be in the way?

LARRY. Of course you won't be in the way. Jill, fix a chair for Dolly. (*Turns to group.*) This is Mrs. Dibble. She's going to play Lady Macbeth.
DOLLY. (*Waves.*) Hi, fellow thespians. (*Crosses to Jill's chair and sits.*)
LARRY. Dolly played the mother for us in "Majority of One" and broke all attendance records. Aside from being our star, she is also our board president, benefactress, and charming hostess.
DOLLY. Oh, you're too much, Larry. (*Indicates dog.*) You don't mind my bringing Rock Hudson with me do you? I couldn't get a dog-sitter.
LARRY. Just so he doesn't bark.
DOLLY. You hear that, Rock Hudson. You be a good dog now. (*To Jill.*) How have you been, dear? I haven't seen you since "Rain."
JILL. (*At her side.*) Well, it isn't every day a good whore role turns up.
DOLLY. And you were just perfect. Emerson won't let me play a whore. (*Rises and crosses c. to Larry.*)
JILL. Pity.
DOLLY. Silly, isn't it? He's dear but square. (*Looks around in feigned horror.*) Oh, I'm holding things up!
LARRY. Not at all.
JILL. It's all right. We were still looking for witches as you came in, Mrs. Dibble.
DOLLY. Well, you go right ahead, Larry dear. I don't want to be in the way. I'll be quiet as a mouse. You'll never know I'm here. (*Scampers coyly back to Jill's chair.*)
LARRY. (*Jumps off stage into aisle again.*) Let's go on, folks. (*Points to Clara Matthews, a girl who had previously raised her hand.*) Did you want to read next, dear? (*Clara rises from u. c. chair and starts down to face Larry below footlights. She wears thick glasses and a muffler around her neck. She sniffles.*)
DOLLY. (*Whispers.*) That's Clara Matthews, isn't it?
JILL. Do you know her?
DOLLY. Her mother does my hair.
LARRY. (*To Girl.*) Do we have your name, dear?
CLARA. (*Inaudibly.*) 'Arrow 'a-who (*Clara Matthews.*)
LARRY I'm sorry, dear, I couldn't hear you.
JILL. (*Looks at her list.*) Clara Matthews. I have it,

LARRY. Have you had any experience, dear? (*Adds quickly.*) In the theater?
CLARA. (*In a soft voice that cannot possibly be heard.*) Ad hool ah aid uh abbot id ahurs id udder-and. (*At school I played a rabbit in "Alice in Wonderland."*)
LARRY. Would you speak up, dear? What did you say you'd done?
CLARA. (*With even less projection.*) Ad hool ah aid uh abbot id a-whose id udder-and. (*At school I played a rabbit in "Alice in Wonderland."*)
JILL. She says she played the rabbit in "Alice in Wonderland."
DOLLY. I couldn't understand a word she said.
LARRY. Oh. Well, would you like to read for us? (*Girl nods shyly.*) Read the role of the second witch in the very first scene. We'll just want to get some idea of tonal quality. From the top, Jill.
JILL. (*Hands her the script.*) I'll read both the other witches, dear.
CLARA. Ah hink ah awed hex-ain. Ah otta code. Ah odd oudda ed du um oder akoss ah ona ee uh akutz. (*I think I ought to explain. I've got a cold. I got out of bed to come over because I want to be an actress.*)
LARRY. You what dear?
DOLLY. I don't know what she's saying. Do you have a speech impediment, or do you talk that way all the time?
JILL. She said she thinks she ought to explain. She says she has a cold. She got out of bed to come over here because she wants to be an actress.
LARRY. Oh. Well, do you feel up to reading?
CLARA. Oh, ess. (*Oh, Yes.! Sneezes.*)
LARRY. Bless you!
EVERYONE ON STAGE. Gesundheit!
JILL. Well, here we go. (*Reads.*)
   "Thunder. Lightning. Enter three witches. First witch.
   When shall we three meet again
   In thunder, lightning, or in rain?"
(*Stops and looks at Clara who says nothing.*) That's your cue. (*Crosses* D. *to her and points to page.*) Here.
CLARA. 'Ere? (*Here?*)
JILL. Yes.

CLARA. (*Stares at it.*) Ud eye ead id oder earst? (*Could I read it over first?*)
DOLLY. *What's* that poor child saying!
LARRY. What, dear?
JILL. She said could she read it over first.
LARRY. Oh. All right. (*Clara takes an interminable time.*)
DOLLY. (*Calls across stage to Effie.*) Hello, Effie. I didn't see you when I came in. How's your sinus? (*Effie shrugs and tries to shush her.*)
LARRY. (*After a wait.*) It's only one line, dear.
JILL. Are you ready now? (*Clara nods. Jill reads quickly.*)
"When shall we three meet again
In thunder, lightning or in rain?"
DOLLY. (*Calls.*) Effie, how about lunch Tuesday. Oh, I'm sorry.
JILL. (*Repeats.*)
"—in thunder, lightning or in rain?"
CLARA.
"Odd uddy am id ad?
Ee an erort, ad emul—"
JILL. (*Interrupts.*) No, Clara—you're reading the *King's* speech. (*Points to book.*) You're the *second* witch.
CLARA. Ad odd it? (*Is this it?*)
JILL. No—that's not it.
CLARA. Ah erdus. (*I'm nervous.*)
LARRY. (*Tartly.*) Show her the *place*, Jill!
JILL. I *did*. She says she's nervous.
LARRY. Everyone's nervous at first, Clara. Try again.
CLARA. Ud eye ead id oher earst oo? (*Could I read it over first, too?*)
JILL. She wants to read it over first, too.
LARRY. Didn't you look at the script before? (*Clara shakes her head.*)
JILL. There's not enough copies to go around.
LARRY. All right. Look at it first.
DOLLY. (*Calls to Effie.*) I'll meet you at noon at the Cozy Cup. (*Effie puts a warning finger to her lips.*)
LARRY. Is anything wrong, Clara?
CLARA. Ah and ee airy ell oz eye ides awe odderin. (*I can't see very well because my eyes are watering.*)
LARRY. What?

JILL. (*Loudly.*) She said she can't see very well because her eyes are watering!
LARRY. You don't have to yell. I can hear.
DOLLY. (*Calls across to Effie.*) Is twelve-thirty all right? (*Effie nods with a pained expression at the interruption.*)
JILL. Clara, your line is:
"When the hurly-burly's done,
When the battle's lost and won."
Are you ready? (*Clara nods.*)
"First witch. When shall we three meet again.
In thunder, lightning or in rain?"
CLARA. (*Shouts.*)
"Hen ee urlyurly un
Hen ee attle's ost ang un."
LARRY. (*Quickly.*) Thank you, Clara. That was perfect. If you'll just wait, please, we'll let you know at the end of auditions whether we can use you.
MARY LOU. (*Rises.*) May I make a suggestion, Mr. Rencher?
LARRY. Of course, Miss Steiner. (*Comes down to stage steps,* L.)
MARY LOU. First—we don't have to be so formal here, do we?
LARRY. What do you mean?
MARY LOU. Close friends call me Lulu.
LARRY. Oh. What is it, Lulu?
MARY LOU. Well, when I directed "Macbeth," we used a couple of boys for witches. As you surely remember, Shakespeare never used women anyhow. And in Scene Three Banquo says to the witches, "You should be women. And yet your *beards* forbid me to interpret that you are."
LARRY. Yes—I remember. But we have more women than boys.
MARY LOU. I just thought I'd help. I hope you don't mind.
DOLLY. I think it's a wonderful idea. (*Crosses to Mary Lou.*) I'm Dolly Dibble. Who are you?
MARY LOU. Mary Lou Steiner.
DOLLY. Do I know you?
MARY LOU. (*Sweetly.*) You do now. My father is *Sheriff Steiner*.
DOLLY. (*Delighted.*) Not *Stinky* Steiner!
MARY LOU. (*Archly.*) His name is Hubbard.
DOLLY. Not when I knew him, dear. Larry, her father is Stinky Steiner. I knew him in grammar school. Of course I was much younger than your father. Tell me, does he still *stutter?*

MARY LOU. (*Coldly.*) No—he *belches* now. You can't do both.
DOLLY. (*Laughs gaily.*) Well, I'm glad to see *someone* in the family is witty. Do say hello for me. Are you going to be with us?
MARY LOU. I'm third witch. But I hope to move up.
DOLLY. (*Pats her hand.*) How nice. You must get your father to tell you how he got his nickname. (*To rest of cast.*) He caught a skunk and brought it to school—
LARRY. Dolly—*would* you mind if we went on with auditions? There isn't much time and—
DOLLY. I'm sorry. I'm sorry. (*Pulls Mary Lou toward Jill's chair.*) Come sit here beside me, dear. (*To Larry.*) It's all right, isn't it?
LARRY. Of course. (*To Jill.*) I think we'll read murderers next.
JILL. Good. I'm fed up with witches.
DOLLY. (*Calls across stage.*) Effie—do you remember Stinky Steiner? (*Effie nods.*) *This* is his daughter!
LARRY. Who's here for murderers? (*All the young boys raise their hands.*) Biff—have you looked over that scene?
BIFF. (*Rises and comes* C.) I read it once.
LARRY. Want to try it for us?
BIFF. (*Shrugs.*) Why not?
LARRY. There are three murderers. Why don't you all read together? Will you two boys come down, please? (*Two teenagers join Biff and stand awkwardly beside him. Jill hands them scripts.*) Biff, you read first murderer. (*To next boy.*) What's your name?
BOY. (*Steps forward.*) My real name or my stage name?
LARRY. You've got a *stage* name?
BOY. My old man said he'd cut off my allowance if I used his name.
LARRY. Oh. Well, what's your stage name then?
BOY. (*Proudly.*) Duke Marlboro.
LARRY. Where'd you get that? (*Boy shrugs.*)
JILL. Obviously from a cigarette butt.
LARRY. (*To next boy.*) And what's your name?
BOY. Curtis Hogg. Think I ought to change it?
LARRY. No. It's solid. Now—you take second murderer and Marlboro will read third murderer.
MARY LOU. (*Jumps up quickly.*) Page forty-four—Scene Three. (*Then to Larry.*) Sorry. I'm so used to doing that. (*Sits again.*)
LARRY. It's all right. Jill, will you read Banquo?

JILL. There's a sound effect of horses arriving in mid-scene. (*To Mary Lou.*) Would you mind being the horses' (*Pause.*) hooves, Miss Steiner?
MARY LOU. That's where the action is.
DOLLY. (*Squeals.*) There's just nothing like pure theater!
LARRY. All right, boys. Let's try it. Set the scene, Jill. And read Banquo's voice.
JILL. (*Reads.*) A park, with road leading to the palace. Enter, three murderers. (*To Biff.*) That's you, Biff.
BIFF.
        "But who did bid thee—"
LARRY. (*Interrupts and points to Duke.*) Wait a minute. Would you mind not chewing gum? I'm sure Shakespeare's murderers didn't chew gum.
DUKE. It's not gum, man. It's tobacco.
LARRY. Tobacco!
DUKE. It's the thing now, man.
LARRY. Well, will you spit it out, please?
DUKE. Where?
JILL. Oh, anyone's eye.
MARY LOU. (*Jumps up with a coffee can.*) Excuse me. Here— use this. (*Crosses quickly with can, Duke spits into can which Mary Lou promptly hands to Jill.*)
LARRY. Thank you, Lulu.
MARY LOU. Any time. (*Leans against proscenium.*)
LARRY. Now. Start again.
BIFF. (*Reads.*)
        "But who did bid thee join with us?"
(*Taps his foot as he reads. There is a wait. Mary Lou prompts Duke.*)
MARY LOU. That's *you*, cutie. "Who did bid thee join with us?" (*Points to Duke.*)
DUKE. Oh. (*Reads his one line.*)
        "Macbeth."
CURTIS.
        "He needs not our mistrust, since he delivers . . . "
BIFF.
        "The west yet glimmers with some streaks of day:"
DUKE.
        "Hark! I hear horses."

JILL. (*To Mary Lou.*) That's you. (*Mary Lou pats both her thighs in imitation of horses' hooves.*) Thank you. (*Reads.*)
"Give us light there, ho!"
CURTIS.
"Then 't is he: the rest
Already are i' the court."
BIFF.
"His horses go about."
DUKE.
So all men do, from hence to the palace gate!
CURTIS.
"A light, a light!"
DUKE.
" 'T is he."
BIFF.
"Stand to't."
(*He spits out the "t".*)
JILL. (*Reads offscene.*)
"It will rain tonight."
(*All the boys look up for rain.*)
BIFF.
"Let it come down."
LARRY. (*Explains.*) At this point you all stab Jill. (*They gather gleefully behind Jill and stab her.*)
JILL. (*Recoils and reads.*)
"O, treachery!"
(*Points to floor.*) Dies.
BIFF. (*They all now look up—finished.*) Man— that's wild!
LARRY. But very good. Thank you. If you'll take your seats again, we'll go on.
MARY LOU. You know, if you wanted to, they could double as soldiers.
LARRY. That's a good idea. Thank you.
DOLLY. (*Calls across to Effie.*) Effie—would you mind if Mary Lou had lunch with us? (*Effie nods agreement.*)
LARRY. (*To Jill.*) What's left?
JILL. What indeed.
LARRY. Well, there's the drunken porter.
DOLLY. (*Calls across to Effie again.*) Effie— (*Effie sighs.*) *I'll* pick *you* up.

LARRY. (*To Jill.*) Who's here that could play the porter?
JILL. (*Crossing back to get clipboard.*) Who's here that could play Shakespeare?
LARRY. (*To group.*) Have we got any drunken porters here? (*Two hands go up—one a very young boy.*) Son— you're too young to be a porter—much less drunk. We'll use you as a soldier. They're very young. (*Points to middle-aged man.*) Ralph—didn't you play a drunk for us in "Never Again"?
RALPH. (*Rather swishily.*) Best performance I ever gave.
LARRY. Do you know the porter scene?
RALPH. I just been studying it.
LARRY. Want to take a crack at it?
RALPH. It's now or never. (*Comes down with book in hand.*)
LARRY. Read it straight—don't be drunk.
RALPH. Wish I were.
LARRY. You're only in this one scene. But it's a tour de force.
RALPH. Whatever that is.
MARY LOU. The *literal* translation is *tower of strength*, n'est ce pas?
DOLLY. (*Squeals.*) Oh, that's French, isn't it?
MARY LOU. Oui, oui.
DOLLY. Merci, beaucoup.
JILL. I will do the knocking at the door for you, Ralph. N'est ce pas? That's French, too.
RALPH. Shoot. I'll be shot anyhow. (*Jill knocks on the box. Ralph trembles a little as he reads.*)
"Here's a knocking indeed. If a man were porter of hell-gate, he should have old turning the key."
(*Jill knocks again. Ralph continues.*)
"Knock, knock, knock! Who's there, i' the name of Beelzebub?
MARY LOU. (*Interrupts.*) Larry—may I make a suggestion?
LARRY. Yes?
MARY LOU. You won't mind? I just want to help.
LARRY. What is it?
MARY LOU. Well, when *I* directed at Bennington, I took advantage of the knock to increase tension. Since King Duncan has just been murdered and it hasn't been discovered yet, I felt the knock should be ominous. Not like this.— (*Repeats Jill's knock on proscenium wall.*) That could be a bill collector. But like this— (*She gives three separate, slow ghostly knocks.*)

DOLLY. (*Squeals.*) Oh, I think that's *wonderful!* (*Squeals.*) Ooo—I wouldn't answer the door.
LARRY. Make it a little more ominous, Jill.
JILL. (*Shrugs.*) You've heard one knock—you've heard 'em all.
MARY LOU. I was just trying to help the actor. You don't mind, do you?
LARRY. Of course not. Go ahead, Ralph. (*Notices book shaking.*) Are you nervous, Ralph?
RALPH. No—that's just a hangover.
LARRY. Take it from "Beelzebub."
RALPH. (*Reads again.*)
"Here's a farmer that hanged himself on the expectation of plenty: come in time:
have napkins enow about you: here you'll sweat for 't."
(*Jill gives three ghostly knocks and nods with a sweet smile.*)
MARY LOU. May I show you? You don't mind, do you, Larry?
LARRY. Go ahead.
MARY LOU. Like this. (*Knocks on back of Effie's chair.*)
DOLLY. Why don't *you* do it, dear?
MARY LOU. (*To Jill.*) Do you mind?
JILL. It's your knuckles.
MARY LOU. Sorry to interrupt you, Ralph. Take it from "sweat for it." (*She knocks her own version on Effie's chair. Effie flinches at each knock.*)
RALPH. (*His shaking intensifies as he reads.*)
"Knock, knock! Who's there, in the other devil's name? Faith, here's an equivocator, that could swear in both the scales against—"
(*At the back of the stage, hammering is heard. Ralph tries to speak over it.*)
"—who committed treason:—"
(*Add his own personal plea.*)
"Enough for God's sake—"
LARRY. Wait a minute, for God's sake. (*Calls.*) Juanito! Juanito!
JUANITO. (*Appears from wings.*) Chess?
LARRY. Will you stop that hammering? We're trying to read out here?
JUANITO. I no doing nothing.
LARRY. You're hammering.
JUANITO. Not me. You esay to me—putting on the heat. You know theez steam pipe? She's hitting herself, I think.

LARRY. Then turn the steam off. It's too noisy.

JUANITO. Ho kay. (*Disappears. They wait a minute for the steam pipes to be shut off.*)

DOLLY. (*Calls across to Effie.*) Effie—I just remembered Tuesday is Election Day. We better stop at my house first for drinks. (*Effie nods agreement with resignation.*)

LARRY. Sorry, Ralph—let's go on.

RALPH. (*The shaking of his papers increases.*)
"—yet could not equivocate to heaven: O come in, equivocator." (*Here Emerson Dibble comes in off the street at the back of the stage with a door bang. They look around.*)

DOLLY. Oh, heavens—it's Emerson. (*Calls.*) Emerson—we're not through! Wait just a minute. (*It is obvious that Mr. Dibble is loaded.*) Sorry, Ralph.

LARRY. Go on.

RALPH. Where was I?

LARRY. "Come in, equivocator."

RALPH. (*Reads.*)
"O come in, equivocator."
(*Mary Lou knocks.*)
"Knock, knock, knock! Who's there?"

EMERSON. (*Cups his hands to call from* U.) The house detective. Get that woman out of your room.

DOLLY. Oh, Emerson—really! Isn't he terrible! Wait a minute, Ralph. (*Crosses to her husband,* U. L.) Emerson Dibble! You ought to be ashamed of yourself.

EMERSON. I'm a bad boy.

DOLLY. You certainly are. (*Pushes him toward door.*) Now, you go out in the car and wait. You're drunk.

EMERSON. (*Nods happily.*) I'm a bad boy.

DOLLY. Go sit in the car. I'll just be a minute. (*Starts back. Emerson tip toes behind her to repeat.*) I'm a bad boy. (*But he scampers out quickly.*)

DOLLY. (*Crosses to her chair,* R.) You'll have to forgive him, Larry. He's been with those drunk Elks all day. You know how he is, Jill. (*Sits.*)

JILL. Yes—he's a bad boy.

LARRY. Go ahead, Ralph.

RALPH. (*Reads.*)
"Faith, here's an English tailor come hither, for stealing out of a

French hose: come in, tailor; here you may roast your goose."
(*Mary Lou knocks.*)
"Knock, knock; never be at quiet! What are you?"
(*Outside, Emerson's insistent horn can be heard honking.*)
"But this place is too cold for hell."
(*The honking continues.*)
DOLLY. Wait a minute, Ralph. (*Goes to door and calls.*) Emerson Dibble, if you honk that horn once more, I'll divorce you.
JILL. He's a bad boy.
LARRY. Sorry about this, Ralph. You want to go back to the beginning?
RALPH. God, no.
DOLLY. (*Calls back from near stage door, U.*) I'll wait here to keep him quiet, Larry.
LARRY. Finish the last few lines.
RALPH. If I can. (*Reads. By this time his trembling is so violent he can hardly hold the papers.*)
"I had thought to have let in some of all professions, that go the primrose way to everlasting bonfire."
(*Mary Lou knocks. He shouts the ending.*)
"Anon, anon! I pray you, remember the porter."
(*Closes book and sighs.*) Made it. (*Hands book back.*)
LARRY. That was great, Ralph.
RALPH. You should have heard my heart knocking. (*Returns to seat. Suddenly the pipes backstage start pounding again.*)
JILL. (*Shouts to pipes.*) You're too late. We're finished.
JUANITO. (*Steps from wings.*) Senor—she no stopping. I keek her and keek her—she no stop. I theenk maybe es something inside she is broke es somewhere I theenk.
LARRY. Get it fixed tomorrow. (*Comes back up on stage.*) Folks, that'll be all for tonight. Thank you so much for showing up. Jill will call those of you we can use tomorrow. You can go out the stage door. And thank you again. I appreciate your patience. Take care, everybody. (*They file out the stage door. The pounding continues intermittently.*)
MARY LOU. (*Follows Larry across to Jill.*) You handle them beautifully—so considerate. It's no wonder they all adore you. You've the patience of Job.
LARRY. Wait'll it's over. They'll hate me.

MARY LOU. I'll be around with a shoulder to cry on. (*Crosses to Jill.*) I hope you didn't mind my knocking for you.
JILL. (*Seated: collecting her papers.*) Let's face it. You have better knockers than I have.
MARY LOU. (*Back to Larry.*) If there's anything else you want me to do—just ask. (*Meaningfully.*) I'll do anything.
JILL. I'll bet.
DOLLY. (*Calls from door.*) Mary Lou, are you coming, dear?
MARY LOU. Mrs. Dibble asked me for a nightcap. Why don't *you* come along?
LARRY. Oh, I've things to clean up here with Jill. (*Goes to get coat.*)
MARY LOU. (*To Jill.*) You wouldn't mind if I stole him, would you?
JILL. Why ask me?
MARY LOU. Well, I assumed—
JILL. (*Rises.*) What? That he hasn't a mind of his own?
LARRY. She was only being polite, Jill.
MARY LOU. I'm sorry if I stepped on your toes, dear. (*To Larry.*) Mrs. Dibble wanted to know her motivation for murder.
DOLLY. (*Sings from door.*) Mary Looo—I'm waiting, dear.
MARY LOU. But *you're* her director.
LARRY. Now, wait a minute. What did she ask you?
MARY LOU. (*Sighs.*) Well—she wants to know what she means when she says, "out damn spot."
JILL. What's the difference? It'll come out the same.
LARRY. Jill, maybe I better go. I don't want Dolly to get off on the wrong foot.
JILL. She got off on the wrong foot when she learned to walk.
LARRY. I'll go for *one* drink. Then I'll come back.
DOLLY. Mary Lou—Dolly Dimple's waiting—
JILL. Don't bother to come back—I have to pick up mother. Maybe father's speaking to her again.
LARRY. You're sure you don't mind?
JILL. Will you please "get thee hence." Or I'll be here all night.
LARRY. Well, good night, Jill. Thanks. (*Gives her a quick peck.*)
MARY LOU. By the way—what is your last name, dear?
JILL. Mudd.
MARY LOU. Oh, you're going to be bags of fun. (*Takes Larry's*

arm as they start out.) When J directed Macbeth—do you know how J wanted to do it?
LARRY. Modern dress? (*Crossing stage.*)
MARY LOU. Nude. Can you imagine that at Bennington?
LARRY. Vividly. (*They laugh and go out with Dolly. The pipes start pounding again.*)
JILL. (*Picking up books.*) Knock, knock. Who's there? (*Crosses c. and looks out.*) Come in equivocator and toast your goose. Methinks this place too cold for hell. (*Calls.*) Juanito!
JUANITO. (*Appears.*) You wanting for me to turning out the lights?
JILL. Yes. (*Hands him her scripts.*) Out! Damn spot. (*She goes quickly out. Juanito studies script as he blows a bubble of gum.*)
JUANITO. (*Reads.*) Dooble, dooble, toil and— (*Stares out at audience.*) Ju knowing somtheeng? I think we have plenty trooble.

CURTAIN

ACT II

Scene 1

PLACE: *The same.*
TIME: *Start of rehearsals.*
AT RISE: *The house lights dim and the stage lights come up.*
The stage is bare. Juanito is again cleaning up the stage. He has the handle of his broom braced in his stomach as he pushes it across thus freeing his hands and shoulders to swing as he sings "La Cucaracha." His uncle, Rodriques, a short little man in work clothes, enters with his girl friend Rosita, buxom and gaudy. They look around, ill at ease.

RODRIQUES. Psst! Psst! (*Juanito, R. fails to hear him as he noisily empties his dust pan. Rosita gives the boy-friend a jab. He cups his hands and calls softly.*) Juanito!
JUANITO. (*Turns.*) Oh, his ju—honcle Rodriques! (*Crosses to them at C. where they lapse into loud, exuberant Spanish. Juanito embraces his uncle warmly.*)
RODRIQUES. Perdone mi tardanza.
JUANITO. Coma esta?
RODRIQUES. Bien. (*Turns to introduce Rosita.*) Juanito—Rosita. Buena amiga mia.
JUANITO. (*Nods.*) Como la va?
ROSITA. (*Touches her chest and coughs.*) Yo tengo catarro.
JUANITO. (*Sadly sympathetic.*) Oh. Lo siento mucho. (*Takes a quick glance at her big breasts, then grins at his uncle.*) Sum keed. (*Rosita gives him a playful slap.*)
ROSITA. Quieres casarte conmigo?
JUANITO. Por que no? (*Takes them over to side chairs, R.*) Venga aca— (*Holds a chair for Rosita.*) Tome esta silla.
ROSITA. Gracias. A que hora acaba el especiaculo?
JUANITO. (*Shrugs.*) Quien sabe? No tenga nervioso. (*He leaves them alone on stage to take a couple of more chairs to the prop*

room. *The two guests sit stiffly and ill at ease. After a moment, Jill enters from the street. She stops and glances across at the strange couple sitting in the wings.*)
JILL. Hello.
RODRIQUES. Buenos noches, Senorita.
JILL. Buenos noches. (*She shrugs and goes about her business. She distributes scripts and proceeds to draw a chalk line in front of the puzzled guests. She then piles two chairs upside down to denote an entrance. She places a waste paper basket below these to represent a cauldron. The two Mexicans watch her, fascinated. After a moment, Larry and Mary Lou come in* L., *through the stage door, arm-in-arm, carrying flowers.*)
LARRY. Oh—You're here early.
JILL. I spent the night.
MARY LOU. Hi, Jill. (*To Larry.*) I'll hang up my coat. (*To Jill, as she starts for dressing rooms,* R.) Dolly said I could share the star's dressing room with her.
JILL. Move right in.
LARRY. (*Forced gaiety.*) Well, I see you've got everything set up.
JILL. (*Chilly.*) I believe you wanted to stage the witches scene first. (*Points to waste basket.*) There's your cauldron for the baboon's blood. (*Busies herself with props and scripts and chairs.*)
LARRY. (*Follows.*) Is anything wrong?
JILL. (*Laughs with mock gaiety.*) Why should anything be wrong?
LARRY. Well, you're kind of chilly.
JILL. My blood hasn't thinned out for summer yet. (*Walks away from him. Larry shrugs and crosses to his Mexican guests who rise quickly.*)
LARRY. Hi, Rodriques. Juanito said he'd bring you. Is this Rosita?
RODRIQUES. Si. Rosita—mi amigo Senor Rencher.
ROSITA. Como esta, Senor?
LARRY. Bien, gracias. (*To Rodriques.*) Do you know anything about rehearsals?
RODRIQUES. Nada.
LARRY. (*Points.*) Well, the chairs are supposed to be the entrance to a cave . . . Some witches are stewing up some trouble. You'll follow it. Make yourself at home.
RODRIQUES. Si gracias—gracias.
LARRY. Por nada. (*Returns to Jill. Sidles up to her confidentially.*) Aren't you going to give us a kiss?

JILL. (*Ignores him.*) It's been so long, I've forgotten how.
LARRY. (*Follows her defensively.*) Look. I've been busy coaching Dolly. You know what a slow study she is.
JILL. Well, Lulu the witch certainly isn't.
LARRY. (*Laughs.*) Ha, ha! So that's what's bugging you.
JILL. (*Stops to face him.*) Am I supposed to feel flattered when you stood me up last week?
LARRY. If you mean having that one drink with them—you *told* me to go.
JILL. Well you know where you can go now. (*Turns away.*)
LARRY. Oh, come on, Jill— You're being a witch yourself.
JILL. (*Faces him again.*) Look, Mr. Genius. Yesterday was my birthday. I reached twenty-five. Safely. A third of my life. I took the day off hoping you'd call. And I aged ten years waiting. That makes me thirty-five. Believe me, it's not the sort of birthday gift that sends a girl into ecstasy.
LARRY. (*Hits his head.*) I wish I were dead!
JILL. Don't tempt me. (*Busies herself straightening chairs.*)
LARRY. Jill—I'm sorry.
JILL. (*Gaily.*) Ooops—I couldn't care less.
MARY LOU. (*Returning.*) Larry, dear—that dressing room smells awful.
LARRY. I know. I wish Dolly wouldn't keep her dog in there.
JILL. (*To Mary Lou.*) Don't worry. Dolly bathes in Chanel. After a few days you'll be grateful to the dog.
MARY LOU. You don't seem in a very chipper mood, Jill?
JILL. It's my arthritis. I'm getting old in a hurry. (*Sits with clipboard, L.*)
LARRY. I hope she doesn't bring that damn dog with her tonight.
JILL. Want to bet? (*The actors start coming in through the stage door.*)
LARRY. Hi, folks. Hi, Sam. (*Points a finger at Effie as she comes down to them, L.*) Effie—you forgot!
EFFIE. What?
LARRY. Your glasses.
EFFIE. No, I didn't. I'm wearing my contacts. (*Other members of the cast start drifting in and stand or sit in background.*)
LARRY. How do you like contacts?
EFFIE. Hate 'em. (*Turns to Jill.*) Hi, Jill. Where have you been lately?

JILL. A good question. (*Larry goes up to talk with another group coming in.*)
EFFIE. Hello, Lulu. You know what happened to me after lunch the other day? I was sick as a dog.
JILL. Wasn't I lucky not to have been invited.
MARY LOU. But wasn't it fun? Dolly's so—so—animated.
EFFIE. I'd be too, if I had her money.
MARY LOU. Effie—Why don't you and I go over our scene together?
EFFIE. Who's the other witch?
JILL. Don't look at me.
MARY LOU. (*Points to Clara at u. with Larry.*) It's that girl over there. I persuaded Larry, she'd fit in with us better.
JILL. I hope she's got over her cold.
EFFIE. (*Looks.*) Small for a witch, isn't she?
MARY LOU. Larry's going to put a hump on her back.
EFFIE. Oh, she'll love that. I adore roles where I have a hump, a limp or a wheelchair.
MARY LOU. What's her name again?
EFFIE. Clara Matthews.
MARY LOU. I'll get her. (*She goes u. to get Clara.*)
EFFIE. (*Turns to Jill.*) Sweet girl, isn't she?
JILL. I've got diabetes. I'm not allowed sweets.
EFFIE. (*Sits beside Jill.*) Is something wrong?
JILL. Now, why does everybody ask me that!
EFFIE. Well, you're carrying such a big sign.
JILL. Oh, Effie—why are men such fools?
EFFIE. Because we make 'em fools. Something gone wrong between you and Larry?
JILL. He forgot my birthday.
EFFIE. (*Pats her hand.*) When you're my age, you'll be grateful.
JILL. I don't mind if I make a fool of him, but Lulu-the-witch is making a fool of him and I resent her improving on my work.
EFFIE. Oh, Jill—she means well.
JILL. For herself.
EFFIE. I hope you didn't remind him he'd forgotten.
JILL. You bet I did.
EFFIE. Then you're a fool, dear. The only way to make a man feel remorse is to be so valiant, he'll hate himself.
JILL. (*Stubbornly.*) It's not as satisfying.

EFFIE. Oh, yes it is. To see a man miserable because he knows he's been a louse, is the most satisfying thing in the world for a woman.
JILL. Well, heaven knows, I'd be happy to see him miserable.
EFFIE. It's hard work but the pay's good. (*Lulu returns with Clara.*) Hello, Clara. How's your lovely mother?
CLARA. *I hate her.*
EFFIE. What's the matter?
CLARA. She's going to get married again.
EFFIE. Really? Who this time?
CLARA. A jerk.
EFFIE. Any jerk we know?
CLARA. (*Points to Horace Mulligan, standing—talking to Larry.*) Him.
EFFIE. (*Looks over.*) Horace?
MARY LOU. You mean the man playing Macbeth?
CLARA. When he gets killed, I'm going to applaud—right on stage.
EFFIE. (*Takes Clara u.*) Well, I think we three witches ought to get together and plan our witches brew.
MARY LOU. Excuse me, Jill—they need my help.
JILL. Whenever you're ready, tell me. I'll start a fire under your cauldron. (*Mary Lou joins Effie u. to go over their lines. Horace comes down and sits beside Jill. He is a gay dog in loud clothes. The rest of the cast wander in and gather in groups in the background.*)
HORACE. Hello, Jill. Am I interrupting anything?
JILL. It's all right. I'm just figuring out how to be valiant.
HORACE. What do *you* think of our doing *Mack* Beth.
JILL. Well, I'm just glad Shakespeare is spared seeing it.
HORACE. I just saw you talking to Clara. I'll bet she had a lot to say.
JILL. She said you're going to marry her mother and she didn't seem happy. I think she needs your help, Horace.
HORACE. The only thing that would help that brat, is a good military school.
JILL. When did this all happen?
HORACE. Well, her mother and I were in this bar—there was a blackout. And one thing led to another.
JILL. You sound like you don't want to get married.
HORACE. Oh, Clara's mother is a fine woman. But Clara's a little odd. (*Rises.*) Her last step-father was poisoned, you know.

JILL. You don't think Clara did it, do you!
HORACE. Well, it's worrisome. A thing like that can spoil your appetite. (*Shakes his head and leaves. The hot water pipes start pounding again.*)
LARRY. Juanito! Turn off that damn furnace. We're going to start rehearsals. (*Comes down to Jill. She rises to meet him.*) As usual, everybody's here but Dolly.
JILL. (*Sweetly.*) It's just inexcusable.
LARRY. Not to her.
JILL. (*Imitating Mary Lou.*) No, I mean the way everyone takes advantage of you. You've the patience of Job, the soul of St. Francis, the heart of a hero and you make pygmies of the rest of us.
LARRY. What the hell's got into you?
JILL. A little soul searching. Is there anything I can do for you, Maestro?
LARRY. Try being your bitchy self. You're much nicer.
JILL. To be or not to be. That is the question. (*Returns to her chair.*)
LARRY. I think we better start rehearsal before I become nauseated. (*Addresses group.*) Will everybody quiet down, please. Mrs. Dibble is late but we're going to start without her. I want to say a word or two first. (*Waits till everyone settles in a circle—some standing, some seated. He goes u. above them to speak.*) Rehearsal will be at seven-thirty every night. Please be on time. If there's an emergency where you can't be here—call Jill—her number is on the call board. As you know, Macbeth is a story of unbridled passions —something none of us here are bothered with, fortunately. I picked "Macbeth" because it has several murders and that usually keeps an audience awake . . . We hope. If you're not in the scene we're rehearsing, please be quiet. If you sit out in the audience, don't smoke—if you want to smoke, go to the green room. But keep quiet. There's a coke machine back there but if it gets stuck, *don't* kick it. Call Juanito to fix it. Where the hell is Juanito anyhow? (*Calls.*) Juanito!
MARY LOU. I'll get him. (*Leaps to her feet and dashes out to be helpful.*)
LARRY. (*Paces.*) Juanito handles the curtain and sound effects. Jill will be on book. I want you to always check your own props when you get them. I don't want a stage wait while you soldiers are looking for your spears. When I block out business, write it in

your manuscript. And, please—no constructive criticism. Any questions? (*There is no answer. Lulu returns with Juanito—a plunger in his hand.*)
JUANITO. The ladies john—she's no working.
LARRY. And girls—you'll have to use the men's john.
JUANITO. She's no got a lock.
LARRY. There's no lock so sing loud or whistle. (*To Juanito.*) I want you to follow business, Juanito—so you'll know where the sound effects are. We have a thunder sheet, don't we?
JUANITO. I'm got heem hop already. (*Shakes the thunder sheet in the wings behind him. Dashes out again.*) You like heem?
LARRY. Good. We're going to set the cauldron scene. That starts with thunder and lightning.
MARY LOU. (*Raises her hand.*) Larry—could I make a suggestion?
LARRY. Yes?
MARY LOU. (*Crosses to him.*) When I did "Macbeth" at Bennington, I opened the witch scene in fog. It created a wonderful spooky feeling of mystery.
LARRY. I don't have a fog machine.
MARY LOU. I'm sure Juanito could make one. It's just a bellows and some dry ice.
JILL. Oh, I think that's brilliant, Lulu. It must have been an inspired production. I'll bet you're a wonderfully inventive director.
MARY LOU. Well, Shakespeare needs a little goosing. (*Crosses back to witches.*)
LARRY. I'll think about it.
JILL. But you'll do it, won't you? You'll get credit for thinking of it. You don't mind if he steals your ideas, do you, dear?
MARY LOU. Of course not. I just want to help.
LARRY. Well, you'll both help me if you'll just let me get on with rehearsals. (*To group.*) Now—as I was saying, Lady Macbeth is late so we'll begin without her. I want to start you on your feet right away. But after this week—no books in your hands. I want you to be letter perfect. All right. Everybody except the witches off stage. (*They all go to the wings, R. and L., to watch. As everyone clears.*) Now. Will our witches please line up behind the cauldron. You'll be discovered there as the lights come up. (*Effie, Clara, and Mary Lou stand behind the over-turned chairs.*)

MARY LOU. Larry, don't you think it would be more interesting if we hobbled in one by one?
JILL. (*Leaps to her feet from her chair,* L.) Of course. It cries out for an entrance singly. Any other way would be wrong. (*To Larry.*) You'll use her suggestion, won't you, Larry?
LARRY. I'll try it. (*Goes to the upside down chairs above the waste baskets.*) Now that's the cauldron—this is the entrance to the cave. First, there'll be thunder and lightning. (*Turns to Juanito.*) You got that, Juanito? You begin with thunder. Always. Understand.
JUANITO. Ho kay. (*Gives loud and long peal of thunder.*)
LARRY Then Effie—you're first witch—and make your entrance.
EFFIE. Shall I cackle when I come in?
LARRY. Not unless you've laid an egg. (*Clara giggles hysterically.*) Just hobble in and come down here center—above the cauldron. (*Demonstrates.*) All right—let's try it. Curtain up. (*Backs to the side.*) Juanito, what are you going to do?
JUANITO. (*Beams.*) Boom-boom-bOOm. I making heem mucho thunder. (*Makes thunder.*)
LARRY. Good. Enter—first witch. (*Effie, shoulders hunched, hobbles down to the waste basket and waits.*)
CLARA. When should I come in?
LARRY. Count four—then follow Effie.
CLARA. One-two-three—
LARRY. (*Interrupts.*) Not out loud! Count four to yourself, then enter. (*Clara counts four silently, then enters to Effie.*)
CLARA. Which side of the pot do I stand on?
LARRY. Stage left.
CLARA. Which is stage left?
LARRY. Left of Effie. (*She stops beside Effie.*) All right, third witch—same count. (*Mary Lou enters and stands to the right of Effie, all above the "cauldron".*) There'll be a pin spot in the cauldron to light up your faces. All right—go ahead, first witch.
EFFIE. "Thrice the brinded cat hath mewed."
CLARA. "Thrice, and once the hedge-pig whin'd."
MARY LOU. "Harpier cries; 'tis time, 'tis time!"
JUANITO. Eez time for more thunder?
LARRY. Not till I tell you. Go on.
EFFIE. "Round and round the cauldron go—"

LARRY. All right—hold it! Here I want you to start circling the cauldron.
CLARA. Which way?
LARRY. Clockwise.
CLARA. Could I write that down, please.
LARRY. (*Nods.*) Yes. Write it down.
CLARA. I haven't got a pencil.
LARRY. (*Hands her his pencil.*) Will everybody please bring pencils. (*Watches Clara scribble.*) Clara—do you wear glasses all the time?
CLARA. Not when I go to bed.
LARRY. Can you see without them?
CLARA. Not very well.
LARRY. Well, I don't think witches wear glasses, dear.
EFFIE. That's why *I'm* wearing my contacts.
CLARA. I can take them off but I bump into things.
LARRY. Well, keep them on for now, dear. Shall we start again? (*Clara starts u. to make her entrance again.*) No, no, Clara! From Effie's line. Go ahead, Effie.
EFFIE. (*Reads.*)
"Round and round the cauldron go."
(*They start circling the cauldron, clockwise.*)
"In the poisoned entrails throw."
(*Makes a gesture of throwing something into the waste basket.*)
CLARA. Excuse me, do I put anything in the pot?
LARRY. Just your talent, dear.
EFFIE. (*Continues.*)
"Boil thou first i' the charmed pot."
ALL. (*In unison.*)
"Double, double, toil and trouble
Fire burn and cauldron bubble."
JUANITO, RODRIQUES, AND ROSITA. (*All three applaud enthusiastically.*) Olé Olé!
LARRY. That's not the end, Juanito! Go on, Clara.
CLARA. (*Reads.*)
"In the cauldron boil and bake
Eye of newt and toe of frog
Wool of bat and tongue of dog."
(*Suddenly Effie screams, hands above her head.*)
EFFIE. Wait! Oh, good Lord! It's gone!

CLARA. (*Looks up.*) That's not in my script
LARRY. Effie—what's wrong?
EFFIE. I've lost one of my contact lenses. (*Kneels and begins slapping the floor around her.*) Don't anybody move! You'll step on it.
LARRY. When'd you lose it?
EFFIE. I don't know. I suddenly realized it was gone when she said "eye of newt."
LARRY. Time out, everybody. Help find Effie's contact lens. Be careful. (*All the actors on stage, with the exception of Clara, Rosita and Rodriques, fall to their hands and knees and like a swarm of ants, start searching helter-skelter on the floor. The Mexican guests sit watching, fascinated as usual.*)
CLARA. Do you need it?
EFFIE. (*Snaps.*) Of course I need it!
CLARA. Lots of witches only got one eye.
EFFIE. We'd make more progress, Clara, if you'd give us a little more help and a little less advice.
CLARA. Why don't we take off our shoes and walk around till someone steps on it?
JILL. Great. All we need is for someone to cut himself and get tetanus.
EFFIE. My eye isn't that poisonous, dear.
CLARA. (*Gets down on her knees.*) I'll look but I don't know what I'm looking for. (*For a moment or two, everyone on stage searches silently crossing back and forth on their knees. The stage door opens and Dolly enters, her dog in one arm, a crutch under the other. She hobbles* D. *with the actors swarming about on the floor. She stops as Effie crawls past her. Effie looks up.*)
EFFIE. Oh, hello, Dolly. (*Biff straightens up long enough to sing "Hello, Dolly." They all groan.*)
DOLLY. What scene is this, Larry?
LARRY. (*Rises quickly upon seeing her crutch.*) Dolly, what happened?
DOLLY. (*Dramatically.*) I fell in the tub. What's everybody doing on the floor?
JILL. We're taking a worms-eye view of "Macbeth."
LARRY. Effie lost her contact lens.
MARY LOU. (*Rises to assist Dolly.*) Dolly, you shouldn't be standing! (*Quickly gets her a chair.*)
LARRY. Is it sprained?

DOLLY. Just twisted.
MARY LOU. Oh, you poor, dear. Sit down. (*Lowers her into chair.*) Does it hurt?
DOLLY. Actually, I don't feel a thing. Emerson made me take a few drinks before I left.
LARRY. You shouldn't have come down at all, Dolly.
DOLLY. Now, don't everybody make a fuss over me. I can rehearse—if you don't mind the crutch.
MARY LOU. (*Pats Dolly.*) You're a real trouper, Dolly.
DOLLY. (*Simpers.*) Well, like they say—the show must go on.
MARY LOU. (*Turns to address the actors.*) Everybody—listen. Mrs. Dibble sprained her ankle but she came to rehearse anyhow. She refused to let us down. I think she deserves a round of applause! (*She leads the applause. The three Mexicans respond enthusiastically—the rest lethargically.*)
JILL. (*In an aside to Effie.*) She should get as much opening night.
DOLLY. Have I missed much? How far did you get?
LARRY. I was just blocking the witch scene.
MARY LOU. You really haven't held up anything, so don't feel badly, dear. (*Clara, kneeling by the waste basket, decides to glance into it. She finds the contact lens and rises with it.*)
CLARA. Is this it?
EFFIE. You angel! (*Rises and takes it.*) I've found it everybody. Thank you. (*Kisses Clara.*) How did you think to look in there? (*Everybody gets to their feet.*)
CLARA. I heard something clink when you threw the frogs leg in.
EFFIE. (*To Larry.*) Excuse me, Larry, I'll go to the little girl's room and put it back in. (*Crosses up R.*)
LARRY. Use the boy's room. The girl's room isn't working.
EFFIE. I only wanted to put my eye back. (*Goes out.*)
LARRY. (*Shouts.*) Take ten, everybody. After Effie gets her eye back in, we'll rehearse Lady Macbeth's sleep-walking scene. (*Everybody rises, begins talking at once and starts for the Green Room, back of the stage. Jill, instead of rising, remains sitting on the floor, L.*)
MARY LOU. Why don't we go to our dressing room where you can rest, you poor dear? I've arranged flowers for you. (*Takes the dog from her.*) Here—let me take your itsie-bitsie baby.
DOLLY. (*Rises on her crutches.*) You're just too too sweet.

LARRY. Are you sure you're not in pain? (*Starts helping her toward dressing room* U. R.)
DOLLY. Not yet.
MARY LOU. (*Crosses* D. *to Jill.*) Jill, dear, do something with Rock Hudson? (*Hands the dog down to her.*)
JILL. Got any ideas?
MARY LOU. You know more about dogs than I do, dear. (*Hurries* U. *to join Dolly.*)
DOLLY. (*As she exits.*) Don't let him talk to any other dogs. He's not a common dog. His ancestors came over on the Mayflower. (*They all exit.*)
JILL. (*Sitting on the floor, glances down at the pooch in her lap.*) It's a dog's life, isn't it? I think I'll bite somebody. (*She sighs and shrugs. Across the stage, Rosita and Rodriques rise and cross to waste basket. They peer down into it in unison. They then look at each other and give elaborate shrugs.*)

BLACKOUT

ACT II

Scene 2

PLACE: *The same.*
TIME: *Ten minutes later.*
AT RISE: *As the lights come up, Larry starts* U. C. *The other members of the cast stand in both wings, and* U. *watching.*

LARRY. Juanito—strike the cauldron.
JUANITO. (*Hurries over.*) You no needing heem no more?
LARRY. Not for this scene. (*Juanito takes the waste basket off.*) Now, this is a room in the castle. The entrance is here—the same as in the witch scene. We're going to do this play with a minimum of scenery. For the audience, it's artistic. For us it's cheaper.
DOLLY. (*She is sitting on a chair* U. C.) Larry, dear—won't there be a throne for me to sit on?
LARRY. No. Nothing.
DOLLY. No benches or chairs?

LARRY. Perfectly bare stage. Nothing to distract. Just the royal drapes.

JILL. (*She sits* U. L.) Burlap.

DOLLY. Where will I sit? I've never known a Queen that didn't sit. It's a royal prerogative.

LARRY. Lady Macbeth is too nervous to sit. You stand.

DOLLY. I've never seen a picture of Queen Victoria where *she* was standing. And she was nervous.

JILL. Dolly, you couldn't sit in the costume I've planned for you, anyhow. (*Rises and crosses to chair* D. L.)

DOLLY. What if my ankle suddenly gives out Opening Night and there's no place to sit?

LARRY. You can lean on your Lady-in-Waiting. You're supposed to be faint anyhow. Now, when the lights come up, the doctor is pacing the floor. Doctor Goldman, will you stand here to pace the floor, please. (*Doctor Goldman, a professional dentist, in a business suit, rises from his chair* D. R.)

DOCTOR. (*Speaks with a thick Jewish accent.*) Vots my attitute, Larry?

LARRY. Concern for the Queen.

DOLLY. No one has the slightest concern for me. If they had, I'd have a throne.

MARY LOU. Larry—couldn't there be something vague up there— (*Points.*) —something that could be a stump for the witches scene and a throne later on?

LARRY. Jill—make a note of that.

JILL. (*Writes.*) One royal stump for the Queen.

LARRY. (*Looks over the group.*) Who's the Queen's Lady-in-Waiting? (*A large teenage girl, better cast as a girl wrestler, holds up her hand.*) Oh, yes. Come over here, dear.

DOLLY. (*In a stage whisper.*) Jill, don't make the throne too high. I don't want to have to *climb* up on it.

JILL. (*Writes.*) One short-legged throne.

LADY-IN-WAITING. (*Crosses* D. *to Larry.*) Do I like the Queen or do I want to kill her, too?

LARRY. Whatever you feel, you don't show it.

LADY-IN-WAITING. That'll take some acting.

LARRY. Now go over there and stand watching the doctor as he paces.

LADY-IN-WAITING. Got it. (*Makes an "OK" sign and crosses to stand beside Dr. Goldman.*)
LARRY. Dolly, do you want to come up here and take your place for your entrance?
MARY LOU. Are you sure you're up to it, dear?
DOLLY. (*Rises on her crutch and takes her position above her entrance, between the two overturned chairs.*) Where's my candle?
LARRY. You won't need props now, Dolly.
DOLLY. I work better if I get used to props. Somebody get me something for a candle.
LARRY. Juanito!
DOLLY. Just so I have something that passes for a candle. I have to believe what I'm doing.
JUANITO. (*Sticks his head out.*) Si?
LARRY. Get the Queen something that looks like a candle stick.
JUANITO. Ho-Kay. (*Disappears.*)
DOLLY. Opening night, will it be a real candle or one of those flash-light things?
LARRY. Whichever you want, Dolly.
MARY LOU. (*Standing beside Dolly.*) A real candle is more dramatic, Dolly.
DOLLY. It won't throw ugly shadows on my face, will it?
JILL. It wouldn't dare. (*Juanito comes in with a short staff with streamers hanging from the end.*)
JUANITO. Theez Ho-kay? Sheez all I got.
JILL. (*Takes it from him.*) That's ideal. A cat of nine tails! (*Hands it to Dolly.*) Your Royal candle, Your Royal Majesty.
LARRY. Do you want Jill to hold your book and read your lines for you?
DOLLY. No—no. I don't want any special favors. (*Turns to Mary Lou.*) Lulu, will you go out to my car for me? There's a silver flask in the glove compartment. It says "To Dolly Wolly from her bad boy." Will you bring it in, please. (*To Larry as Lulu runs out.*) If the pain is too much, I'll have to take a little painkiller. Do you mind?
LARRY. Of course not. Maybe we better put a chair out here and just have you sit and read your lines.
DOLLY. I wouldn't hear of it. If I feel faint, I'll lean on— (*Turns to her Lady-in-Waiting, standing* R. *with Dr. Goldman.*) What's your name, dear?

LADY-IN-WAITING. You always ask me that.
DOLLY. Well, who are you?
LADY-IN-WAITING. Your Lady-in-Waiting.
JILL. Her name is Dixie Delaney.
DOLLY. I never heard of a Lady-in-Waiting being called Dixie.
LARRY. I think the Delaneys have taken the house next door to you, Dolly.
DOLLY, Oh, the people with the tom-cat. Will you speak to your mother about that cat? It persists in using my rose bed.
LADY-IN-WAITING. Put out some kitty litter.
MARY LOU. (*Returning with a flask.*) There was a box of candy, too. You didn't want that, did you?
DOLLY. No, dear. But would you mind getting me a cup. I think it's so common to drink out of a flask.
JILL. Dixie—get her a Dixie cup.
MARY LOU. (*Eagerly.*) I'll get one.
DOLLY. You know, if I had a daughter, I'd want her to be like Mary Lou.
JILL. That's probably what you'd get. (*Crosses L. to sit.*)
LARRY. (*Quickly.*) Now, Dolly, on your entrance, come right down center stage and stare vacantly out over the audience. (*Demonstrates.*) It'll be very effective. Play your whole scene there.
DOLLY. I don't sit down?
LARRY. No—just stand there until "to bed, to bed, to bed." Then turn and walk slowly out. You'll probably get a hand on your exit so take your time.
DOLLY. Do I turn and take a bow?
LARRY. No—you're sleep-walking. You don't hear it.
MARY LOU. (*Returning with a glass.*) This is all I could find. Juanito had a paint brush in it but I washed it out.
DOLLY. Thank you, dear. (*Pours a sizable drink.*) I'm sorry I have to do this. (*Gulps it down.*)
LARRY. It's too bad you had to fall just as we're starting rehearsals.
DOLLY. Excuse me. (*She pours another drink.*)
LARRY. Are you sure you're up to this, Dolly?
DOLLY. Oh, I can handle twice as much.
LARRY. I mean—the scene.
DOLLY. Oh, that. Yes. Shall we go on?
LARRY. Are you feeling any pain?

DOLLY. (*Happily.*) Not a thing. (*Hands flask back to Lulu.*) Hold this for me, dear. I may need it later. Don't go far away.
LARRY. All right. Places! Quiet everyone. (*He goes down in the audience to watch. Mary Lou moves back, leaving the principals at* C. *Dolly hobbles* U. *to wait for her entrance cue.*) Lights up. The Queen's chamber. Start pacing, Doctor Goldman.
DOCTOR. (*Starts pacing back and forth, reading from his book. Dixie stands, twisting her hands.*)
"I have two nights watched with you—"
DOLLY. (*Shouts.*) Wait a minute! (*Points to Dixie.*) Is she going to twist her hands like that?
LARRY. I wasn't watching. Why?
DOLLY. Well, I have to come in and twist my hands. I don't think we should *all* be twisting our hands.
LARRY. Dixie—just stand watching.
DIXIE. O.K. Look, no hands. (*Puts them behind her back.*)
LARRY. Go on, Doctor.
DOCTOR.
"I have two nights watched with you but can perceive no truth in your report. When was it she last walked?"
DIXIE. (*Reads with elaborate hand gestures.*)
"Since his Majesty went into the field. I have seen her rise from her bed, throw her nightgown upon her, unlock her closet, take forth a paper, write upon it, read it, afterwards seal it, and again return to bed. Yet all this while in a most fast sleep."
DOCTOR.
"A great perturbation in nature, to receive at once the benefits of sleep and do the effects of watching!"
DOLLY. (*Calls to Mary Lou.*) Lulu—will you look in my purse—you'll find a breath spray. Will you bring it to me please?
DIXIE.
"That, sir, which I will not report after her."
DOCTOR.
"You may to me. And tis most meet you should."
(*Lulu tiptoes to Dolly and hands her the spray.*)
DIXIE.
"Lo, you! Here she comes!"
LARRY. That's your entrance, Dolly!
DOLLY. Just a minute! (*She sprays her throat.*) Thank you, dear. Could I have the cue again, please.

LARRY. "Lo, here she comes." (*Dolly comes slowly* D. *on her one crutch, the whip in one hand, her book in the other. She stops and stares out over the audience, suppressing a hiccup. Dixie continues.*)
DIXIE.
"—This is her very guise and upon my life, fast asleep. (*Points.*) Observe her. Stand close."
DOCTOR. (*To audience.*)
"How came she by that light?"
DIXIE.
"She has light by her continually—tis her command."
DOCTOR. (*To audience again.*)
"You see—her eyes are open."
(*Actually, they are almost closed. She opens them quickly.*)
DIXIE.
"Aye—but their senses are shut."
(*Dolly weaves a little.*)
DOCTOR.
"What is it she does now? (*To audience.*) Look, how she rubs her hands."
DOLLY. (*Hobbles toward Larry and speaks over footlights.*) Larry dear, I'll *have* to have something to put the candle on if I'm going to rub my hands! I *can't* hold a lighted candle between my knees.
LARRY. All right—there'll be a chair or a stump or something there for the candle.
DOLLY. It's got to be a throne. I wouldn't have a stump in my bedroom.
MARY LOU. Larry. I used a pedestal when I did it. It's easier to strike between scenes.
DOLLY. I don't know why you can't think of those things yourself, Larry. You're the director. (*Returns* C.)
LARRY. All right! All right! There'll be a pedestal.
DOLLY. In the meantime, will someone hold my candle while I wash my hands.
LARRY. Put it on the floor, Dolly!
DOLLY. Will you *stop* barking at me? After all I'm doing this for you on crutches.
LARRY. I'm sorry. Someone hold her candle.
MARY LOU. (*Jumps up and runs to her.*) I'll do it. (*Takes the "candle."*) Poor Dolly—to have to endure this. You're so brave.

DOLLY. Thank you, dear. (*To* Dixie.) Well, give me my cue. You're a Lady-in-Waiting, but you don't have to wait!
DIXIE. (*Shouts.*)
"It is an accustomed action with her, to seem thus washing her hands."
DOLLY. (*Glares down at her outstretched hand.*)
"Yet here's a spot."
(*Crosses toward Larry in the audience.*) I hate that line, Larry. Everybody in the audience is going to think I have liver spots
MARY LOU. (*Sweetly.*) Dolly, I think if you read it this way— "Yet here's a—" hesitate—then "spot!" they'll know it's new to you.
JILL. Oh, Lulu—that's wonderful. You're so clever. You always put your finger right where it belongs.
MARY LOU. Well, it seemed obvious.
DOLLY. Not to Larry. (*Returns* C.)
LARRY. *Shall* we go on, please?
DOLLY. I've lost my momentum. Can we go back?
LARRY. All right, Dolly. Where do you want to go back to? Genesis?
DOLLY. Are you being sarcastic, Larry?
LARRY. Of course not. Where do you want to go back to, Dolly?
MARY LOU. Why don't you take it from "Her eyes are open."
DOLLY. They certainly are. Thank you, dear.
DOCTOR. Is that my line?
LARRY. You're the doctor.
DOCTOR. (*Reads.*)
"What is it she does now."
LARRY. *What* are you doing *now*, Dolly.
DOLLY. I'm taking off my rings to wash my hands. (*To Mary Lou.*) Will you hold them, dear. They're the biggest diamonds in town. (*To Doctor.*) You don't have to stop for me, Doctor Goldman.
DOCTOR. (*Reads.*)
"Look how she rubs her hands."
DIXIE.
"I have known her to continue in this a quarter of an hour."
DOLLY.
"Yet here's a—spot!"

DOCTOR. (*To audience.*)
"Hark! She speaks. I will set down what comes from her."
(*Pretends to write.*)
DOLLY.
"Out! Damned spot! Out, I say!"
CLARA. (*From u. l. comes a loud outburst.*) Oh, shut up!
DOLLY. (*Stunned.*) Who said that?
LARRY. Who said that?
CLARA. I did. (*Points to Horace. Both are u. l.*) He's not my father yet so tell him to shut up!
LARRY. What's all this about? There's a rehearsal going on here!
CLARA. Then make him shut up.
DOLLY. I'm going to lose my mind. Get me my medicine, Lulu. (*Mary Lou hands her the flask. She drinks.*)
LARRY. What's wrong here, Horace! (*Comes on stage to quell the disturbance above Dolly.*)
HORACE. I don't know. I just asked her why she didn't get her teeth straightened like her mother asked her to.
CLARA. Oh, shut up. (*Dolly's dialogue plays over the dialogue going on behind her. Everyone seems to be talking at once.*)
DOLLY. Do we rehearse or do we fight over someone's teeth? (*Takes another swig.*)
LARRY. (*To Clara.*) Look—if you have any personal arguments to settle—don't settle them here while I'm rehearsing.
DOLLY. (*At the same time.*) My nerves are hanging out—raw and bleeding! (*Takes another drink.*)
MARY LOU. Sit down, Dolly, while Larry tries to maintain order.
DOLLY. I can't. There's no throne!
MARY LOU. Just relax, dear.
DOLLY. No throne. No discipline! No Dixie cups!
HORACE. (*Simultaneously over Dolly's scene.*) I'm sorry, Larry. The kid's all uptight on account of her mother and me. I just asked about her teeth and she flared up.
CLARA. (*Yells.*) Oh, shut up!
LARRY. Clara—this is very unprofessional.
CLARA. Then tell him to shut up!
DOLLY. Lulu—see if you can do anything before I'm a nervous wreck. (*Mary Lou crosses to Clara.*)
HORACE. OK OK—I'll shut up! Cripes!
MARY LOU. Clara, dear, why don't you come with me. (*Pulls

her toward Green Room.) I'll treat you to a coke, and let you pet Rock Hudson.

HORACE. (*Shouts after her.*) Get her teeth fixed up while you're about it.

CLARA. (*Screams back at him.*) Oh, shut up! (*They go out. Larry crosses back D. to Dolly.*)

DOLLY. You really ought to exercise more authority with your actors, Larry. Look at my hand shake.

LARRY. Dolly, when people are acting for nothing, you can't use a whip. I'm sorry for the interruption.

DOLLY. All I can say, it's lucky Lulu is here.

JILL. Oh, she's a lulu, all right.

LARRY. Let's go on. *Quiet everyone!* Where were we, Doc? (*Goes back into audience to watch.*)

DOCTOR.

"Hark, she speaks."

(*Steps forward.*) You know, Larry, speaking as a dentist, that girl really should let me straighten her teeth.

LARRY. I'll straighten them for her if she does that again.

DOLLY. Are we going to rehearse or not!

LARRY. Start your speech again, Dolly.

DOLLY. (*Exhales a martyr's sigh.*) I've got a splitting headache. (*Reads.*)

"Out, damned spot! Out, I say!

Tis time to do it."

(*Turns to Larry.*) Do *what*, Larry! I don't understand this speech. What am I supposed to *do!*

LARRY. Kill the King.

DOLLY. But he's already dead.

LARRY. You're dreaming it all over again.

DOLLY. Oh. You see how confused you've got me. (*Reads.*)

"Fie, my Lord, fie!"

(*To Larry.*) What the hell does *"fie"* mean!

LARRY. Shame.

DOLLY. Why doesn't she say shame then? How's the audience going to understand this play if I don't understand it myself?

JILL. (*Seated L.*) They've read it.

LARRY. Say whatever you want, Dolly. Fie—shame—darn—I don't care.

DOLLY. "Shame, my Lord, Shame! Who would have thought the

old man to have have so much blood in him!" (*To Larry.*) Do I look down at the blood?
LARRY. Step in it if you want to.
DOLLY. Larry, I don't think you're showing the proper attitude to Shakespeare—not to mention me.
LARRY. Then will you please just read your lines, Dolly, and let me tell you what to do? Go ahead, Doc.
DOCTOR. (*Reads.*)
"Do you mark that?"
DOLLY. (*Glares at Larry but continues.*)
"The Thane of Fife had a wife—where is she now?"
DOCTOR.
"Go to, go to—you have known what you should not."
DIXIE.
"She has spoke what she should not.
Heaven knows what she has known."
DOLLY.
Here's the smell of blood still—"
(*At the stage door, a swarthy Spanish workman enters and starts a loud argument in Spanish with Juanito.*)
LARRY. Quiet!
DOLLY.
"Here's the smell of blood still, all the perfumes of Arabia will not sweeten this little hand. Oh. Oh. Oh."
(*Hurls her book on the floor.*) Oh, for God's sake stop that noise!
LARRY. Juanito—we're rehearsing. *Who is that man?*
JUANITO. Heez de hozband of Rosita. (*Points to Rosita. Both she and Rodriques try to hide behind Dr. Goldman.*)
LARRY. Well, what does he want!
JUANITO. He wants for keel her. (*At this Rosita screams and flees to Dolly. She falls on her knees and hugs Dolly's legs.*)
ROSITA. Hees goan for keel me. I doan do nothin'. He keel me. No let heem keel me, pliz! Oh, Madre de Dios! (*Rodriques proves that discretion is the better part of valor by running down the steps and fleeing up the aisle, after being chased around the stage.*)
RODRIQUES. (*Running up the aisle.*) Policemans! Policemans! Eez in here a keeler. Policemans! (*He disappears into the lobby.*)
DOLLY. I'm going mad. I'm going stark raving mad. (*Rosita's husband starts toward her. Juanito tries to hold him back by the seat of his pants with the help of Horace.*)

LARRY. Get him out of here, Juanito. (*To the boys watching.*) You! Soldiers! Help throw that maniac out. (*They start toward the struggling pair.*)

ROSITA. (*Still on her knees, clinging to Dolly's legs.*) Heez got a knife! He keel you.

DOLLY. (*To Rosita.*) Let go of me! Can't you see I'm crippled. (*Stares heavenward.*) I'm going right out of my mind. (*Larry and Juanito and the soldiers manage to pull the struggling husband to the door.*) Will someone get this serpent off me!

MARY LOU. (*Returns from pacifying Clara.*) What's going on?

DOLLY. (*Screams.*) Where's my Baby! What's happened to Rock Hudson!

MARY LOU. It's all right, Dolly. He's tied in the wings.

DOLLY. (*Looks down at Rosita.*) Let go of my feet, you Spanish octopus.

MARY LOU. (*To Jill.*) What happened anyhow?

DOLLY. Someone tried to kill someone. A madman came in with a knife. (*To the sobbing Rosita.*) You're getting my feet wet! (*Juanito and Larry manage to get the husband out. Larry comes back panting to Dolly D. C.*)

LARRY. I shouldn't have let them come in to watch.

DOLLY. *You* invited them?

LARRY. They're friends of Juanito.

DOLLY. Well, that's the last straw. How dare you subject me to this humiliation. I came here on my death bed and you show me no consideration. You have no control over the cast and—

LARRY. *Oh, shut up!* (*There is a stunned silence.*)

MARY LOU. Larry—who do you think you're talking to!

JILL. Lady Macbeth.

LARRY. (*Shouting.*) I've had about as much as I intend to take. I'm through. (*To Mary Lou.*) *You* want to direct this play? Direct it! (*To Dolly.*) And as for you, you cup of curdled cranberry yogurt—you can take your damned candle and you know what you can do with it. (*Rosita, still hugging Dolly's legs, wails suddenly.*) Oh, shut up! (*He storms out of the theater, hurling his script to the floor. There is a stunned silence.*)

JILL. (*Grins.*) "Who would have thought the old man to have so much blood in him." (*She throws her script down and follows Larry gleefully out.*)

CURTAIN

ACT III

Scene 1

PLACE: *The same.*
TIME: *Technical Rehearsal and Picture Call.*
AT RISE: *The stage is bare. During the intermission, chairs, tables and a waste basket have been removed by boys and girls acting as stagehands.*

When the house lights go down and the stage lights go up, the concentrated activity on stage begins. A pre-set twelve-foot ladder is D. L. Juanito is on top to set the lights, with only his behind showing. Two boys (or girl stagehands) bring a roll of drapes and kneel to tie them to the lowered pipes R. Two more bring down a six-foot platform and place it against the pipe for the drapes U. C. These are already attached. They then throw a cloth over it to represent the stump or throne. They then carry in a roll of drapes D. L.

DUKE. (*Enters from R., stepping over drapes. He looks up into the grid above.*) Hey fatso. Get off your can and let the pipes down for the drapes stage left. (*The pipe is lowered. Jill enters, looking rather harried.*)
JILL. (*To Duke.*) Duke, where's Lulu?
DUKE. Who cares?
JILL. Well, she's the director now. She should check what you're doing.
DUKE. I know what I'm doing.
JILL. Where's Juanito?
DUKE. Above it all. (*Points to the ladder. Jill crosses D. to the ladder.*)
JILL. Juanito?
JUANITO. (*Pops his head down from the top of the ladder.*) Ju calling for me?
JILL. How long will it take you to set lights?
JUANITO. I no know teel I feenish.

JILL. (*Shrugs helplessly.*) Ask a foolish question. We have to take pictures. Will we be in your way?

JUANITO. Ju no be in the way of me honless ju coming hop here.

JILL. Do the best you can. (*Crosses back to Duke and Curtis Hogg, the two boys tieing drapes at* R.) How long will you boys be?

DUKE. How many days till Christmas?

JILL. (*Points to the covered box.*) Is that the throne?

CURTIS. In the castle scene, it's a throne; in the cave scene, it's a stump.

DUKE. And in the battle scene, it's a pain in the ass to get off.

JILL. My dear boy, we do not use such language here.

MARY LOU. (*Comes in from the rear* R., *and addresses the boys kneeling, hooking on drapes.*) You, whoever you are—didn't you hear me calling?

DUKE. I didn't hear anybody calling, who-ever-you-are. (*To others.*) Did you?

MARY LOU. (*Extends a bill.*) I want you to run over to the drugstore and get some aspirin. Dolly has a headache.

CURTIS. (*Rises.*) I'll go. I want to get a malted.

DUKE. Get me one.

THORTON. (YOUNG STAGE HAND) Me, too. Chocolate. With strawberry ice cream.

CURTIS. (*As they all dig down for money.*) You want anything, Jill?

JILL. Nothing they sell in a drug-store, dear. (*He starts off.*)

MARY LOU. Wait. Will you get me a spray can of *Pine Air Freshener*?

CURTIS. Air freshener?

MARY LOU. Rock Hudson threw up in Dolly's dressing room. (*Curtis shrugs and goes out,* L.)

JILL. (*To Mary Lou.*) I'm glad I caught you. You can tell Duke how you want the drapes hung.

MARY LOU. You do it dear. I'm rubbing Dolly's neck. (*Starts off* R.)

JILL. Well, what about the picture call. Have you got your list ready?

MARY LOU. List of what?

JILL. The shots you want. Haven't you made it out?

MARY LOU. Oh, that. Can't you attend to it, dear?

JILL. Don't you want to stage the sound effects?

MARY LOU. With Dolly in such pain? You do it.
JILL. But you're the director.
MARY LOU. I trust you. (*Starts out again.*)
DUKE. Hey! Miss-who-ever-you-are.
MARY LOU. (*Turns to him scornfully.*) Such a witty boy for a mongoloid.
DUKE. (*Gleefully.*) I just wanted to know—did you have to clean up after Rock Hudson?
MARY LOU. No, dear. I just threw the rug out for *you* to clean. (*She goes off.*)
DUKE. You know, I'll bet she did.
JILL. I'll say this. She's made *one* terrific change here. Morale is shot to hell.
DUKE. (*Camping.*) My dear girl, we do not use such language here.
JILL. I never realized before how good Larry was.
DUKE. For two cents, I'd quit. But nobody's made an offer.
JILL. Well, you fellows hang the drapes and let her hang herself. (*To another boy.*) Thorton, will you tell the army to come on stage and bring their trumpets?
THORTON. (*Races off* R., *yelling.*) To arms! To arms! The British are coming!
JILL. (*Crosses down to Juanito.*) Juanito?
JUANITO. (*Sticks his head down to see her.*) Si?
JILL. Could you stop long enough to set a sound level for the trumpets?
JUANITO. Ho-Kay. (*As he climbs down, Duke rises and calls offstage.*)
DUKE. (*Cupping his hands to call up in the flies.*) Off your can, Fatso. Pull up the right tormentor. (*The right drape starts up, masking off that side of the stage.*) That's good. Tie it off there!
JILL. (*To Juanito.*) Did you get the tape I ordered with the sound of trumpets?
JUANITO. Si. Ju want for hearing heem?
JILL. Would you put it on, please. You'll have to take a sight cue. Can you see us from the wings?
JUANITO. Si. I see.
JILL. Then set it up, please.
JUANITO. Ho-Kay. (*He goes off* R.)
JILL. Thorton! What's happened to the army?

THORTON. They're cleaning up after Rock Hudson.

JILL. Tell them I need them on stage. (*Thorton disappears.*)

DUKE. (*Calls off-scene.*) Oh, lover—you can pull up number three pipe now? (*They stand watching as the pipe goes up. A crude large coat-of-arms has been painted on this drop.*)

JILL. Duke, dear. You've hung it wrong. The coat-of-arms is upside down.

DUKE. Oh, piss! (*He sinks down dejectedly on the throne.*)

JILL. Duke! You want me to tell your mother the kind of words you use here?

DUKE. She knows them. (*Shouts.*) Bring up the tormentor, left. Let's see if that's right. (*While the tormentor, L., rises, Juanito comes on to put down a loudspeaker, on stage.*) Tie it off!

JUANITO. (*Returns to look at drape.*) Sheez hopside down, I theenk.

JILL. It's all right. We're playing this scene on our heads. (*As Juanito exits, the army, led by Biff, enters from behind the drapes R. It is probably the most disreputable army of three ever assembled. They carry toilet plungers as trumpets from which banners hang. On their heads are metal mixing bowls for helmets. Their coat-of-mail is made from the tabs off the tops of beer cans and under this, they are wearing ill-fitting, dyed red long underwear.*)

BIFF. Well, here we are—the King's men.

JILL. You know something. I think you'd look better naked.

BIFF. We'll scare hell out of the enemy.

JILL. Well, let's fix you up. First, pull up your underwear. Especially in the back. And for heaven's sake, wear jock straps.

THORTON. (One of the soldiers.) My coat-of-mail keeps coming apart.

JILL. You'll have to be careful. It's made with the tabs off the tops of beer cans and we're running short of beer.

BIFF. Some army, aren't we? Pancho Villa rides again.

JILL. I wouldn't let you in the army of the unemployed. (*Calls.*) Juanito—can we try the sound of trumpets now?

JUANITO. (*In wings.*) Ho-Kay.

JILL. (*To soldiers.*) Go off stage left and line up for your cue. Come in on, "Hail, Thane of Glamis." Face front and bring your trumpets to your lips and pretend to be blowing. *In unison!* Juanito will coordinate the sound of trumpets. (*To Juanito.*) You got that, Juanito?

55

JUANITO. Ho-Kay. (*Disappears.*)

JILL. (*To soldiers.*) All right. Go out stage right and stand by. (*They start out* R.) Stage right is thataway, fellas. (*They march out.*)

CLARA. (*Sticks head thru center drapes.*) Jill, where are the witches wigs?

JILL. Ask Lulu! (*Clara's head disappears. Jill calls to Biff.*) Ready, army?

BIFF. (*Offstage.*) Ready.

JILL. (*To Juanito.*) Ready, Juanito?

JUANITO. (*Offstage.*) Ho-Kay.

JILL. "Hail, Thane of Glamis!" (*The three bedraggled soldiers march in, out of step, reach* C. *and face front. They bring their trumpets to their lips. There is a great peal of thunder.*) Juanito!

JUANITO. (*Steps out.*) Ees sometheeng wrong?

JILL. Yes—ees something wrong. We want the sound of trumpets—not thunder.

JUANITO. Oh! I fixing heem. (*Disappears.*)

JILL. And let's hear the trumpets—good and loud. (*To boys.*) All right fellas, ready? "Hail, Thane of Glamis!" Trumpets up! (*They wait and wait.*) Juanito! What's the matter. Let's hear the trumpets!

JUANITO. (*Comes onstage.*) Ju know es-socket? Ju know de plog wot goan een de es-socket. I forgetting to put her een heem already.

JILL. Well, plug in your machine and let's hear trumpets!

JUANITO. Ho-Kay (*Goes out.*)

JILL. (*To soldiers.*) All right kids—get set. Ready? Trumpets up! (*The boys swing their trumpets up to their lips in a flourish. Behind them, the drapes part and Curtis sticks his head in to shout.*)

CURTIS. I've got your malted milks!

JILL. Not now! Wait! (*They stand frozen—waiting. Nothing happens.*) Juanito! What's wrong? (*Curtis hands Duke his carton of malted milk and exits. Duke sits watching from the throne, sucking his malted thru a straw.*)

JUANITO. (*Sticks his head out of the wings.*) Eez something go wrong?

JILL. Yes, eez something go wrong. What happened to the sound of trumpets?

JUANITO. Ju es-say—"Not now." Ju es-say "Wait."

JILL. No, no! I *want* the trumpets now. I don't want the *malted milks* now!

JUANITO. Ju know sometheeng? I no got no malted milks.
JILL. Once more, *please*. (*Juanito backs out.*) Ju know sometheeng? This show's never going to get on without Larry.
DUKE. I saw him last night at the Purple Pig. Pissed.
JILL. (*Loftily.*) And what were *you* doing in a *bar*? And don't use that word.
DUKE. I was trying to find my old lady.
JUANITO. (*Sticks head out.*) Ju ready?
JILL. Si, Senor. Ready. (*He goes out.*) All right, boys. One for the money, two for the show, three to make ready, four to go. Go! (*They whip their trumpets up. A blast of trumpets is heard thru the speaker, loud enough to wake the dead. The entire army flinches. Duke falls to the floor, covering his ears.*)
DUKE. (*Leaps up on "throne"*) We've broken the sound barrier! Eureka!
BIFF. Man—that was a blast.
JILL. I wonder if it's too late to become a nun?
JUANITO. (*Sticks his head out.*) Ho-Kay?
JILL. Sorry, I can't hear you, Juanito. My ear drums are busted. (*To soldiers.*) Thank you, boys. That's all, Biff—if the witches are ready, tell them to come on stage so I can check their costumes. We have to take pictures, you know.
BIFF. (*Gallops off.*) All right, Army! The enemy's coming. Desert! Surrender! (*They scramble good-naturedly out.*)
JILL. Juanito—it was just a teensy-weensy bit loud. Give us half that volume. After all, you're not Gabriel and the world hasn't ended. (*Adds.*) Yet.
JUANITO. Ho-Kay. I poot heem down. (*Goes out.*)
JILL. (*Crosses up to Duke.*) Duke, did you talk to Larry last night at the Purple Pig?
DUKE. I told you—he was (*Spells.*) P-I-S-S-E-D.
JILL. Will you *stop* using that word.
DUKE. What you getting so uptight about? He was. Pissed. (*He sucks on the straw, making an irritating gurgle.*)
JILL. You know, you're not going to get the last drop unless you eat the carton.
DUKE. (*Rises and saunters off* L.) O.K. If I bug you, call me when you want the drape switched. (*Jill is left alone for a minute.*)
JILL. (*Looks heavenward.*) Oh, Larry, if you only knew how we needed you. Come back, little Sheba. (*The* u. *drapes part and Effie*

comes in wearing her witch outfit. There is no doubt about her being a witch.)
EFFIE. Well, how do you like my new Easter outfit? It's a Dior. That's short of deodorant.
JILL. I love it. You remind me of my Aunt Sophie.
CLARA. (*Enters.*) What about me? You think this hump is too big? (*Turns around revealing a lump that has slipped down to her posterior.*)
JILL. Not for a camel.
CLARA. It itches.
JILL. That's all right. You can scratch. Witches scratch.
CLARA. That's funny. My mother is always yelling at me to stop scratching.
JILL. Be Actors Studio. Make it part of your performance.
EFFIE. You'll probably win an Oscar.
JILL. Where's our third witch?
EFFIE. Rubbing Dolly's neck. She said you could do without her.
JILL. Prophetic words. Well, you two look all right. Who made your wigs?
CLARA. My Grandma. It's just wool yarn she didn't want. Moths got in it.
JILL. They look it.
EFFIE. You're doing all of Lulu's work, Jill.
JILL. I'm just rehearsing for a new role—Christian martyr.
EFFIE. Where's the photographer?
JILL. That's about number eighty-six in things I don't know.
CLARA. You want me any longer?
JILL. I'd like you a little taller. But you can go. Thank you, dear. Remember—scratch.
CLARA. I do anyhow. I got a monkey on my back. (*She goes out, leaving Effie alone with Jill.*)
EFFIE. Is Mary Lou really going to be our director all next year?
JILL. If she can stop rubbing Dolly's neck.
EFFIE. You know, dear—I try to like everybody—but there's just something about that girl that rubs me the wrong way.
JILL. Move over. (*The drapes part and Larry leans in.*) Psst—Jill.
JILL. Larry! (*Runs to him and holds him fondly.*)
EFFIE. There! You see. There *is* a Santa Claus.
LARRY. Could I see you a moment, Jill?

JILL. (*Suddenly pushes him away, angrily.*) Why haven't you called me? What were you doing at the Purple Pig?
LARRY. Paying my bill. I'm leaving tomorrow.
JILL. Leaving. Where for? I mean for where?
EFFIE. Larry—You can't fly off and leave us to flounder alone. It's a shambles, boy.
LARRY. Isn't Lulu working out?
JILL. All she does is sit on her duff while Dolly guzzles and Rock Hudson throws up.
EFFIE. We need you, Larry.
LARRY. Not a chance. Effie, could I talk to Jill alone?
EFFIE. (*Sighs.*) Nobody loves a witch. (*Pause.*) Except a he-witch! (*Goes to drapes.*)
LARRY. Don't tell anybody I'm here.
EFFIE. Do *I* look like someone who couldn't be trusted? *Yes.* (*Goes out.*)
JILL. What do you mean—you're leaving?
LARRY. I'm going to New York. I can stay with my folks. Then I'll try for a job in summer stock.
JILL. You can't abandon us like that. You can't be a sinking rat.
LARRY. I've been fired, Jill. There's nothing here for me.
JILL. There's *me*.
LARRY. Once I land something, I'll send you a ticket.
JILL. Send me a marriage license. (*Throws her arms around him.*) Oh, Larry, I love you so much my teeth hurt.
LARRY. Well, naturally, we'd have to get married if we're going to live with my mother.
JILL. (*Hugs him.*) Oh, you're beautiful. (*Eric, an attractive young man with a camera, comes thru the drapes. He watches the embrace from above them for a moment.*)
ERIC. Excuse me.
LARRY. Eric!
ERIC. Is that part of the play or are you just playing around?
LARRY. Eric—meet my bride. She just proposed to me.
ERIC. Then you must be Jill.
LARRY. This is Eric, Jill. My buddy from Amherst.
JILL. Oh, the photographer. (*Shakes hands.*) You do theatre photography, Larry tells me—summer stock.
ERIC. A little pornography on the side. I couldn't interest you, could I?

JILL. Only on Sunday. Are you going to take pictures for us?
ERIC. That was the general idea.
LARRY. Eric—since I last talked to you, I've been fired. If you don't want to take pictures, it's up to you.
ERIC. Gee—I'm sorry.
JILL. Oh, please take them. It would do our morale so much good.
ERIC. Some of my shots have just the opposite effect.
JILL. (*Starts* u.) I'll get Lulu for you. She's our new director.
LARRY. I'll meet you later, Jill.
JILL. Oh—don't go.
LARRY. It's too embarrassing.
JILL. (*Points.*) Look—get up on the ladder. They'll think you're Juanito.
LARRY. All right. But remember—you haven't seen me. (*Jill exits.*)
ERIC. I like her. What happened?
LARRY. (*Goes to ladder.*) I just got fed up. You know, Eric, there are three sexes—male, female and actors.
ERIC. What else is new?
LARRY. So I'm going to try my luck back East. (*Climbs up ladder. Eric stands at the foot talking to him.*)
ERIC. If you think it's any better back there—you're nuts.
LARRY. At least they're professionals.
ERIC. All that means is—they get paid. (*Lulu comes in.*)
MARY LOU. You wanted to see me?
ERIC. (*Turns to face her.*) Yes. I wanted to know— (*Stares at her.*) Say! You're Bobo Hepburn, aren't you?
MARY LOU. (*Stiffens.*) I'm afraid you've made a mistake.
ERIC. Westport. Summer stock. You've done something to your hair.
MARY LOU. (*Archly.*) My name is Mary Lou Steiner. I've *never been* to Westport.
ERIC. You got a sister?
MARY LOU. Not that we know of. What can I do for you?
ERIC. (*Grins.*) The same as you did in Westport.
MARY LOU. I've told you. I've never been to Westport. I'm sorry. I'm not this other girl.
ERIC. (*Looks at her, leering.*) So am I. Are you sure you haven't got a sister?
MARY LOU. I'll ask father. He's the *sheriff* here, you know.

ERIC. (*Backs up.*) Oh, well in that case, I never saw you before, Miss Steiner.
MARY LOU. I assure you, you never have. Now, as I said, what can I do for you?
ERIC. Well, I told Larry I'd take some shots for him. But since he's not here, can you line up your people for me?
MARY LOU. I'll have Jill take care of you. I'm *very* busy. Excuse me. (*She goes out. Eric stares after her until Larry calls from the top of the ladder.*)
LARRY. Eric. (*Starts down.*) You think you've met Lulu before?
ERIC. I know I have.
LARRY. How do you know?
ERIC. (*Grins.*) Oh, come on.
LARRY. (*Goes up to him.*) Was she acting at Westport?
ERIC. She sure was. In the *box office*.
LARRY. But she was a drama major at Bennington.
ERIC. She was an *apprentice* at Westport.
LARRY. But why would she call herself Bobo Hepburn?
ERIC. She's a pathological liar. She claimed she was Katherine Hepburn's cousin, too.
LARRY. Could you prove she's the girl you knew there?
ERIC. It wouldn't be easy.
LARRY. Why?
ERIC. Well, she's got this birthmark.
LARRY. Where?
ERIC. (*Whispers to him.*) See why?
LARRY. You rascal! (*Thinks.*) I've got an idea. (*Goes to ladder.*) Hand me that loud speaker. (*Starts to climb up ladder. Eric hands him the speaker box used for trumpets* D. C. R. *against proscenium.*)
ERIC. What are you going to do?
LARRY. Play a new role—the voice of conscience.
ERIC. You've got an Equity card?
LARRY. (*From top.*) Hold the ladder. I want to hide this out of site. (*Hides speaker above trim.*)
ERIC. She's a real mixed up dame, you know. She was always claiming to be pregnant, raped or dying of leukemia. Usually in that order.
LARRY. (*Comes down ladder.*) Well, I'm going to add to her repertoire. Help me strike this. (*They push the ladder out of sight.*)
ERIC. Aren't you going to let me in on the plot?

LARRY. You'll be in for the kill. Lady Macbeth isn't the only one to hear voices. (*Goes out behind drapes,* R.)

JILL. (*Enters* C.) Where's Larry?

ERIC. I wish I knew.

JILL. Lulu said you wanted me.

ERIC. Madly. But for openers, can we get started on the pictures?

JILL. Who do you want to start with?

ERIC. Let's shoot Lady Macbeth first. She's your star, isn't she?

JILL. (*Goes to* D. *drapes.*) If temper tantrum and no talent makes you a star—she's a star. (*Goes out thru drapes. Eric puts bulbs in his camera and focuses his lens. In a moment, Dolly and Jill return. Dolly is in her sleep-walker gown, which trails out some length behind her.*) Dolly—this is Eric Howe, our photographer from back East.

DOLLY. (*Extends her hand.*) Oh, must you take pictures of me! I always look ten years older. Where do you want me to sit?

ERIC. What scene is this?

JILL. The sleepwalking scene.

ERIC. Let's have you standing against the drapes. They're upside-down, aren't they?

JILL. I'll get it fixed. (*Calls.*) Duke Marlboro!

DOLLY. You mean I have to *stand* here waiting while someone fixes the drapes?

JILL. You can sit on your throne, Dolly. (*Which she does, draping her train behind her with a kick of her foot.*)

DUKE. (*Enters.*) I know. I know. The drapes are upside down. (*Calls up into the flies.*) Fatso—lower the upstage pipe. (*The rear drapes descend behind Dolly.*)

DOLLY. I'd like you to take a few extra shots of me. My husband wants them for his office. I'll wear my crown.

JILL. Dolly—you're sleepwalking. You wouldn't go to bed in your crown.

DOLLY. If I'm sleepwalking—I don't know what I'm doing.

JILL. (*Shouts.*) Curtis! Bring the Queen's crown!

DOLLY. Why isn't Lulu here?

JILL. Maybe Rock Hudson threw up again. (*To Eric.*) That's her dog, in case you wondered.

ERIC. I did.

CURTIS. (*Comes in with crown.*) We haven't put the gems in it yet. Thorton's gone to the Five and Dime for diamonds.

DOLLY. (*Takes crown.*) Can't anybody here do anything right? (*Examines crown.*) Is there a front to a crown?
JILL. No—it's like an egg. You've seen one side—you've seen it all.
DOLLY. (*Puts her crown on.*) It wobbles. Someone should have measured my skull. I don't know why I tolerate such inefficiency.
JILL. (*Curtseys.*) Because you're every inch a Queen, Dolly.
DOLLY. Dignity is something from within. Now where the hell is my candle? I'm supposed to be holding a candle. (*Points to a soldier eating a popsicle u.*) You—whoever you are, get me my candle. Tell Lulu to bring it herself. (*The boy dashes out. Dolly addresses Eric.*) She's my director. I want her with me. I demand loyalty.
JILL. That's talking like a Queen.
DOLLY. Jill, if you're being funny, your humor is lost on me.
JILL. I'm lucky.
DOLLY. Do you want to focus me, young man?
ERIC. What's your good side?
DOLLY. Full face. I lose something in profile.
JILL. Everybody does. One eye.
DOLLY. Jill, could you spare me your wit?
JILL. Sorry. I haven't got any to spare.
DOLLY. You're being deliberately rude because of Larry and don't think I don't know it.
MARY LOU. (*Enters.*) Here's your candle, Dolly, dear. Where do you want it?
JILL. Don't answer.
DOLLY. (*Glares at Jill.*) Thank you. I'm ready now. (*Lulu starts to leave.*) No—Lulu. You stay here. I can't trust anyone else.
MARY LOU. You don't need me, Dolly, dear, so if I—
DOLLY. (*Imperially.*) I need you. I want you here.
JILL. The Queen hath spoken.
MARY LOU. Of course, dear.
ERIC. Well, looks like we're all set when we get the drapes up.
JILL. Are you finished, Duke?
DUKE. (*Rises with his hammer and calls. He is grinning impishly.*) Oh, sweetheart—raise the Royal Tapestry. (*The drapes start going up. Dolly stands, crown on, against them holding her candle. Slowly, the train on the back of her gown starts going up with the drapes. Duke, aware of what he has done, suppresses his mirth.*

The curtain starts pulling Dolly's gown up behind her. Next it starts pulling Dolly backwards. Note: Please test fly rope with excess weight. We don't want to lose an actor.)

DOLLY. Stop him. Somebody—I'm caught. Help. Lulu! I'm going up!

ERIC. Oh, man—what a shot. *(He snaps one after the other, dashing right and left of Dolly.)*

MARY LOU. Somebody—stop the curtains.

DOLLY. Help—help. *(If possible, she should be pulled up on the curtain and suspended in mid-air. Otherwise, her dress is pulled up under her arm, rendering her helpless.)* Do something, somebody! Jill—do something.

ERIC. *(Takes a picture.)* This is going to make a hell of a picture for her husband's desk.

DOLLY. Someone did this on purpose, Lulu. Why don't you help me! *(Above, over the loudspeaker, an ominous voice is heard.)*

VOICE. This is the voice of Conscience. Confess that you are Bobo Hepburn, alias Mary Lou Steiner—with a birthmark you-know-where. Repent! Deny to the world that you are pregnant, raped or dying of leukemia. Harken to the trumpets of Judgment Day, Lulu.

MARY LOU. *(Turns on Eric.)* You beast. You dirty double crossing pig. *(Beats him with her fists as he backs off.)* You told them!

DOLLY. Lulu! Let me down! Let me down! *(She whirls helplessly.)*

JILL. I think she already let you down, Dolly.

DOLLY. Help. Help. Emerson—wherever you are! Help! *(As the trumpets blare forth—the lights dim.)*

CURTAIN

ACT III

Scene 2

PLACE: *The Same.*
TIME: *Opening Night. Shortly before curtain time.*
AT RISE: *During the blackout, the actors have cleared. When lights come up, Emerson Dibble, in dinner jacket and carrying a large bunch of flowers, is seen stumbling alone about the stage in a drunken stupor.*

EMERSON. Dolly! Dolly! Where's my Dolly Wolly. I've come to wish you a Happy Opening Night night. (*Beats against the drapes, trying to find an opening.*) Dolly—come help me. I'm trapped! How the hell did I get in this nun's laundry line. (*He staggers up to glare at the center drapes.*) Anybody back there? (*Turns and stumbles to footlights.*) Anybody out there? (*Looks up to heaven.*) Anybody up there? (*Duke and Curtis part the drapes and carry the cauldron to c. This is nothing more than a large plastic clothes basket or trash can painted and padded to somewhat resemble a cauldron. Emerson stumbles over to the boys.*) Where'd you come from?

DUKE. Horace Mann Junior High.

EMERSON. Who are you? (*Crosses between them.*)

CURTIS. I'm his brother, sir.

EMERSON. (*Points back to Duke.*) Who'd you say you were?

DUKE. His father.

EMERSON. (*Stares at cauldron.*) Oh. What's that?

CURTIS. A pot.

EMERSON. What's cooking?

DUKE. Witches brew.

EMERSON. Is it good?

DUKE. If you like frog legs, dogs tongues, newt's eyes, baboons blood and fillet of snake. (*They start out.*)

EMERSON. Wait a minute. Where's my wife?

CURTIS. Is she a witch?

EMERSON. I guess you don't know *who I am*.

CURTIS. I guess you guessed right, sir.

EMERSON. I am Emerson Stillwater Doolittle Dibble. How's that for a name?

DUKE. It's all right, if you like it, sir.

EMERSON. (*Draws himself up proudly but with difficulty.*) I own this building. (*Stands on platform.*)

CURTIS. The john doesn't work, sir.

EMERSON. (*Mumbles.*) I own three cars and a thirty foot sloop. Named Dolly.

CURTIS. Has it got a dinghy?

EMERSON. She's got two dinghys. (*Slurs drunkenly.*) I own the finest house on Pussywillow. Four baths.

DUKE. Pays to play safe.

EMERSON. And five acres. You know what I've only got one of?

DUKE. I wouldn't want to say.
EMERSON. I've only got one wife. (*Getting maudlin.*) But she's the most beautiful wife this side of Pussywillow. You know what I want?
DUKE. An *Alka-Seltzer*?
EMERSON. (*Tearfully.*) A son. I have no one to carry on the name of Emerson Stillwater Doolittle Dibble. (*He pulls Duke's head under his arm and pats him drunkenly on the top of the head. Duke winces. Curtis sneaks out* U. C.)
DUKE. You're hurting my ear, sir.
EMERSON. (*Releases Duke.*) All I got is a little dog. A little, *little* dog. (*Demonstrates as Duke escapes unnoticed.*) I hate that dog. It stinks. You want a good dog? (*Turns to find them gone.*) Some day I'm going to *sit* on that little dog and that'll be the last of *that* little dog. (*Sits to demonstrate.*) Dolly! Dolly! (*Larry comes in quickly. He is also wearing a tuxedo for the opening.*)
LARRY. What's going— (*Sees Emerson.*) Oh, it's you, Mister Dibble.
EMERSON. (*Trying to focus his eyes.*) Who are you? (*Rises.*)
LARRY. It's me. Larry. You know me, Mr. Dibble.
EMERSON. (*Sneers.*) Are you accusing me of not knowing who my friends are?
LARRY. Mister Dibble—the audience will start coming in in a few minutes. We're getting ready for a performance. You can't come backstage.
EMERSON. I happen to own this building. I want to wish my wife a Happy Opening Night night. Tonight! (*Repeats for clarity.*) *Night* night.
LARRY. I'll see that she gets your flowers, Mister Dibble. Please go out front.
EMERSON. No, you don't. (*Backs off platform.*) You'll give them to somebody else. (*Starts shouting again.*) Dolly! Dolly! (*The drapes part, and Dolly enters in her regal robes, majestic in her anger. She crosses* D. *to him.*)
DOLLY. Emerson Stillwater Doolittle Dibble! This is outrageous!
EMERSON. (*Cowed.*) You're mad.
DOLLY. How dare you come backstage as I'm about to go on!
EMERSON. I'm a *bad* boy.
DOLLY. You're a drunken sot.
EMERSON. I'm a *bad* drinken sot.

DOLLY. If you don't get off this stage, this instant, I will have you thrown off.
EMERSON. *(Hands her the bouquet of flowers.)* For you. *(Begins to sing.)* "Happy Opening Night night to you. Happy Opening Night night to you. Happy Opening Night night Dear Dolly"— *(At this point the call boy crosses stage giving the warning call.)*
THORTON. Five minutes. Places. Five minutes. Five minutes. *(Goes out.)*
EMERSON. *(Finishes.)* "Happy Opening Night night to you."
DOLLY. *(Throws the flowers into the cauldron.)* Larry, call the army. Throw him out.
EMERSON. Ahh—you threw my flowers away. *(He reaches in to retrieve his bouquet and falls forward. When he struggles to his feet, the container is around his shoulders, making him look like Humpty-Dumpty. This cauldron should just fit snugly around his shoulders.)*
DOLLY. It's too much. It's simply too much. *(She faints conveniently onto the platform behind her as Emerson stumbles about with the cauldron on his head, almost going into the footlights.)*
LARRY. *(Shouts.)* Jill! Jill!
EMERSON. Dolly! Dolly! Where are you?
LARRY. Biff! Juanito! Thorton! Anybody! *(He straddles Dolly and pats her hand. Jill enters.)*
JILL. Larry—what are you doing to Dolly?
LARRY. She's fainted, damn it. Don't just stand there.
EMERSON. *(Going in wrong direction.)* Dolly—Dolly!
JILL. Who's that?
LARRY. Emerson Stillwater Doolittle Dibble! Damn it! *(The call boy returns and crosses stage.)*
THORTON. Five minutes. Five minutes. Five minutes. *(Exits.)*
LARRY. Where is everybody! Biff! Horace!
JUANITO. *(Enters and looks around.)* You know something? I theenk maybe the curtain she woan go hop.
LARRY. Help Jill.
BIFF. *(Enters.)* Something wrong? *(Others come in to watch.)*
JUANITO. Somebody sheez fall in de pot?
JILL. Biff—hold his legs. Juanito, we'll pull on the pot. *(Emerson falls to his knees. They get the cauldron off his shoulders. Emerson looks up.)*
EMERSON. I'm a bad boy. *(He promptly passes out.)*

BIFF. He's passed out.
JILL. (*Turns to the army, who have come in on the excitement.*) Boys—take him outside. (*They put the bouquet on his chest and lift him by his arms and legs, off the floor and start out with him.*)
BIFF. What'll we do with him?
JILL. If you've got a truck—run over him.
BIFF. We'll lock him in the girls' john.
JILL. (*Looks down at him as they carry him out.*) Goodnight, Sweet Prince.
LARRY. Jill, help me with Dolly! (*He starts slapping Dolly to revive her.*)
JILL. Be careful. You'll knock her crown off.
DOLLY. (*Opens her eyes.*) Where am I?
LARRY. On stage. You're about to go on.
DOLLY. Ohhh— (*She promptly faints again. Biff returns.*)
LARRY. Dolly! Wake up.
EFFIE. She fainted again. Slap her.
CLARA. Let *me* slap her. I'll wake her.
LARRY. Clara—get some water to throw on her.
DOLLY. (*Quickly sits up.*) No—no! You'll ruin my dress. (*Grasps Larry's hand.*) Oh, Larry—I can't go on. I'm shattered. My nerves are gone. Look! (*Extends a trembling hand.*)
LARRY. Biff—get her flask. And call the entire company on stage. (*Biff goes off.*)
DOLLY. It won't do any good. Cancel the performance. My career is ended. (*Starts crying.*)
LARRY. (*Shouts.*) Like hell I will. Get to your feet. You're going to go on. And stop crying, do you hear me
JILL. You're ruining your make-up.
DOLLY. I can't! I can't!
LARRY. All right! (*Crosses to Effie R.*) Effie! Do you think you know the part well enough to go on *instead of Dolly*.
DOLLY. (*Rises quickly.*) No—no! I'll go on. I may die as the curtain descends but I'll go on. I won't let Shakespeare down. (*Crosses to Larry.*) Oh, Larry, whatever I do tonight—whatever I am—I owe to you. You created me.
LARRY. God, I hope not. (*Larry goes to stand on platform as actors assemble on stage. Horace comes in in costume with a helmet on with horns, looking more like "Brünhilde." Dr. Goldman has on a hood with a long grey beard. The porter is in tights with a plume*

on his cap. The others are equally ill-dressed. Larry turns to address them.) It's all right everybody. We've had a little confusion but everything is under control. We're going to give a hell of a show. We've just got a minute but I want to take that time to thank all of you for your loyalty and cooperation. All over this country—in high schools—and regional theatres, plays are being put on by groups like ours. I sometimes wonder how they ever get on but they do. And I hope they always will. It's a tribute to man's enduring spirit and blind tenacity. So get through this tonight as best you can. Get through life as best you can. You'll deserve your applause. Now get out there and give a good show. Places! Curtain going up! (*The entire cast applaud. The curtain begins to slowly descend.*)

THE END

PROPERTY PLOT
ACT I

Preset:
  Folding chairs around the stage (at least fifteen)
  Two wastebaskets (D.R. and D.L.)
  Garbage on stage (C.)
  Box with eight coffee cans on stage (D.L.)
  Box and piece of plywood for a table (L.)
  Bench (U.R.)

Offstage:
  Push broom and dust pan (Juanito) R.
  Nine scripts, clip-board, pencil, glasses (Larry) L.
  Two scripts, clip-board, pencil, handbag, hamburger in bag (Jill) L.
  Folding chair (Juanito) R.
  Chewing tobacco (Duke) L.
  Dog (Dolly) L.

ACT II—Scene One

Strike:
  Bench (R. wing)
  Scripts
  Box and plywood

Preset:
  Move chairs U.

Offstage:
  Pushbroom (Juanito) R.
  Clip-board, pencil, script, chalk in handbag (Jill) L.
  Clip-board, pencil (Larry) L.
  Flowers, script (Lulu) L.
  Scripts (each actor) L.
  Dog and crutch (Dolly) L.
  Plunger (Juanito)

ACT II—Scene Two

Strike:
  Dog
Preset:
  None

Offstage:
 Whip (Juanito) R.
 Flask (Lulu) L.
 Dixie cup (Lulu) R.
 Breath spray (Lulu) R.
 Knife (Rosita's husband) L.

ACT III—Scene One

Strike:
 Bench
 All chairs
 All coffee cans
 Wastebaskets
Preset:
 Ladder D.L.
 U.C. Drape
Offstage:
 Tools and paintbrush (Juanito) at curtain
 Platform (Angie and Louise) L.
 Trash can and drop cloth (Angie and Louise) L.
 Right drapes (Curtis and Duke) R.
 Left drapes (Angie and Louise) L.
 $10 bill (Lulu) R.
 Speaker (Juanito) R.
 Three plungers with banners (three soldiers) R.
 Malted milk, straw, paper bag (Curtis) L.
 Crown and popsicle (Curtis) R.
 Candle in candlestick (Lulu) R.
 Three metal mixing bowls (three soldiers)
 Camera and photo equipment (Eric)

ACT III—Scene Two

Strike:
 Dolly
 Candle
Preset:
 Platform D.
Offstage:
 Cauldron (Curtis and Duke) U.C.
 Flowers (Mr. Dibble) L.
 Flask (Biff) R.

NEW PLAYS

★ **THE CIDER HOUSE RULES, PARTS 1 & 2 by Peter Parnell, adapted from the novel by John Irving.** Spanning eight decades of American life, this adaptation from the Irving novel tells the story of Dr. Wilbur Larch, founder of the St. Cloud's, Maine orphanage and hospital, and of the complex father-son relationship he develops with the young orphan Homer Wells. "...luxurious digressions, confident pacing...an enterprise of scope and vigor..." –*NY Times*. "...The fact that I can't wait to see Part 2 only begins to suggest just how good it is..." –*NY Daily News*. "...engrossing...an odyssey that has only one major shortcoming: It comes to an end." –*Seattle Times*. "...outstanding...captures the humor, the humility...of Irving's 588-page novel..." –*Seattle Post-Intelligencer*. [9M, 10W, doubling, flexible casting] PART 1 ISBN: 0-8222-1725-2 PART 2 ISBN: 0-8222-1726-0

★ **TEN UNKNOWNS by Jon Robin Baitz.** An iconoclastic American painter in his seventies has his life turned upside down by an art dealer and his ex-boyfriend. "...breadth and complexity...a sweet and delicate harmony rises from the four cast members...Mr. Baitz is without peer among his contemporaries in creating dialogue that spontaneously conveys a character's social context and moral limitations..." –*NY Times*. "...darkly funny, brilliantly desperate comedy...TEN UNKNOWNS vibrates with vital voices." –*NY Post*. [3M, 1W] ISBN: 0-8222-1826-7

★ **BOOK OF DAYS by Lanford Wilson.** A small-town actress playing St. Joan struggles to expose a murder. "...[Wilson's] best work since *Fifth of July*...An intriguing, prismatic and thoroughly engrossing depiction of contemporary small-town life with a murder mystery at its core...a splendid evening of theater..." –*Variety*. "...fascinating...a densely populated, unpredictable little world." –*St. Louis Post-Dispatch*. [6M, 5W] ISBN: 0-8222-1767-8

★ **THE SYRINGA TREE by Pamela Gien.** Winner of the 2001 Obie Award. A breathtakingly beautiful tale of growing up white in apartheid South Africa. "Instantly engaging, exotic, complex, deeply shocking...a thoroughly persuasive transport to a time and a place...stun[s] with the power of a gut punch..." –*NY Times*. "Astonishing...affecting ...[with] a dramatic and heartbreaking conclusion...A deceptive sweet simplicity haunts THE SYRINGA TREE..." –*A.P.* [1W (or flexible cast)] ISBN: 0-8222-1792-9

★ **COYOTE ON A FENCE by Bruce Graham.** An emotionally riveting look at capital punishment. "The language is as precise as it is profane, provoking both troubling thought and the occasional cheerful laugh...will change you a little before it lets go of you." –*Cincinnati CityBeat*. "...excellent theater in every way..." –*Philadelphia City Paper*. [3M, 1W] ISBN: 0-8222-1738-4.

★ **THE PLAY ABOUT THE BABY by Edward Albee.** Concerns a young couple who have just had a baby and the strange turn of events that transpire when they are visited by an older man and woman. "An invaluable self-portrait of sorts from one of the few genuinely great living American dramatists...rockets into that special corner of theater heaven where words shoot off like fireworks into dazzling patterns and hues." –*NY Times*. "An exhilarating, wicked...emotional terrorism." –*NY Newsday*. [2M, 2W] ISBN: 0-8222-1814-3

★ **FORCE CONTINUUM by Kia Corthron.** Tensions among black and white police officers and the neighborhoods they serve form the backdrop of this discomfiting look at life in the inner city. "The creator of this intense...new play is a singular voice among American playwrights...exceptionally eloquent..." –*NY Times*. "...a rich subject and a wise attitude." –*NY Post*. [6M, 2W, 1 boy] ISBN: 0-8222-1817-8

DRAMATISTS PLAY SERVICE, INC.
440 Park Avenue South, New York, NY 10016 212-683-8960 Fax 212-213-1539
postmaster@dramatists.com www.dramatists.com